The Living Flame

The Living Flame

The Revolutionary Passion of Rosa Luxemburg

PAUL LE BLANC

Haymarket Books
Chicago, IL

Published in 2019 by
Haymarket Books
P.O. Box 180165
Chicago, IL 60618
773-583-7884
www.haymarketbooks.org
info@haymarketbooks.org

ISBN: 978-1-64259-034-0

Distributed to the trade in the US through Consortium Book Sales and Distribution (www.cbsd.com) and internationally through Ingram Publisher Services International (www.ingramcontent.com).

This book was published with the generous support of Lannan Foundation and Wallace Action Fund.

Special discounts are available for bulk purchases by organizations and institutions. Please call 773-583-7884 or email info@haymarketbooks.org for more information.

Cover design by Rachel Cohen.

Printed in Canada by union labor.

Library of Congress Cataloging-in-Publication data is available.

10 9 8 7 6 5 4 3 2 1

CONTENTS

ACKNOWLEDGMENTS

In considering the people who helped me understand Rosa Luxemburg, I should probably begin with Shirley Dorothy Harris, who became Shirley Le Blanc. She was strong, cultured, warm, self-assured and outgoing, highly intellectual, critical-minded, highly principled, drawn to Marxism, dedicated to the cause of labor and to an end to all oppression and violence, animated by an elemental feminism and a belief that each person is worth something and should be treated with dignity. To a significant degree and in more than one way, she prepared me for an appreciation of Rosa Luxemburg—in part as a mother, and in part as a teacher, an example, and a role model. This book is dedicated to her memory.

Among the Marxists who were my teachers and mentors, I think my friend Michael Löwy had the biggest influence on helping me to appreciate aspects of Luxemburg's contributions, but Ernest Mandel was also quite important in this regard. George Breitman—whose early role in Pathfinder Press probably had something to do with the publication of *Rosa Luxemburg Speaks*—also deserves mention.

There are a number of colleagues with whom I have shared the experience of exploring the life and ideas of this wondrous revolutionary. Professor He Ping of Wuhan University has been one of these, helping to open China to me in ways that impacted powerfully on my understanding of Luxemburg and much else. Another Chinese sojourner who has been important to me has been Xiong Min. From Germany the friendship and challenging intellectual companionship of Ottokar Luban have also been a positive influence, in part despite and in part because of our disagreements (though there is much common ground). Kunal Chattopadhyay, Soma Marik, and Sobhanlal Datta Gupta in India are also very much a part of this network. Another Luxemburg soul mate is my friend and comrade Helen C. Scott, with whom I have had the good fortune to compare notes more than once and to co-edit the Pluto Press anthology *Socialism or Barbarism: The Selected Writings of Rosa Luxemburg*.

In the quest to comprehend and to share contributions of Rosa Luxemburg, two insane comrades have had the vision of creating in English *The Complete Works of Rosa Luxemburg* (a project that they sucked me into): a much-missed pal, the late Bill Pelz, and most especially the remarkable Peter Hudis, the keystone of the project. There is also George Shriver, a close political comrade for many years and through many battles, and also a brilliant translator who has been incredibly important in this project. All three of these friends have been with me on the project's editorial board, an entity that has been expanding too rapidly to cite all its individual members. And certainly the publisher of the *Complete Works*, Verso Books, should also be mentioned, and especially staff members Sebastian Budgen, the late Clara Heyworth, and Jake Stevens.

Central to the success of the *Complete Works of Rosa Luxemburg* has been the Rosa Luxemburg Foundation, a German-based but genuinely global entity, just like its namesake. There are too many associated with it to name them all, and to name one or two would be unfair to the others. Their presence and assistance in continuing the work of Rosa Luxemburg has been felt not only in Germany, of course, but also throughout Europe, as well as in the United States, South Africa, Turkey, India, China, and elsewhere.

My profoundest thanks must go to comrades who have sustained Haymarket Books over the years, and especially to the hands-on editing work of Ida Audeh and Rachel Cohen.

Then there is my immediate family, and loving them has been an essential element in my balance, without which I could not have created this volume. Most wondrous are my grandchildren Sophia and Zach, their mother Rima Le Blanc, and their late father Gabriel, my beloved son. Closer to home is my other son, Jonah McAllister-Erickson, and his companion Jessica Benner. There are also my sisters, Patty Le Blanc and Nora Le Blanc, and my dearest loving friend, Nancy Ferrari.

INTRODUCTION

Growing numbers of people throughout the world are coming to know Rosa Luxemburg. Her passion and clarity, her critical and creative intelligence, her strength and courage, and her wicked humor and profound warmth and humanity are qualities that attract many. People are drawn to Luxemburg's analyses and ideas on how reality works and what we can do to overcome oppression and gain liberation, animated by that lively intelligence that is permeated with inspiring values. They are drawn to her penetrating discussion of the relationship of reform to revolution, to her sense of the interplay between revolutionary organization and spontaneous mass action, to her remarkable analyses of imperialism and militarism, to her unshakeable conviction of the centrality of genuine democracy to genuine socialism, and of the compelling need for both. All this and more.

As resistance and insurgency continue to be generated by the crises of our time, people turn to her ideas, and her ideas become more readily available—certainly for those who speak English, thanks to the fact that Verso Books, in cooperation with the worldwide Rosa Luxemburg Foundation, has begun to make available *The Complete Works of Rosa Luxemburg*, a project I have been proud to assist.

As more and more people are engaging with her ideas and life, I want to feed some of my own thoughts into the proliferating dialogue, in part with this collection of essays composed over three decades.

GETTING TO KNOW ROSA LUXEMBURG
I came to know Rosa Luxemburg gradually.

In 1962, when I was fifteen, I got a copy of C. Wright Mills's book *The Marxists*, a mass market paperback, which was an essential initiation in my education as a Marxist.[1] Mills respectfully, if critically, introduced her to me, and shared some excerpts from her writings. He said she had her head in the clouds, and I only half-understood the excerpts from her writings, but I knew this was someone I must get to know better.

Not long after, I found Bertram D. Wolfe—whom I distrusted because he was a Cold War anticommunist and very much an ex-Marxist—giving me his latter-day "take" on her in his 1965 collection *Strange Communists I Have Known* (also a mass market paperback).[2] Far more important for me was Hannah Arendt's surprisingly loving and serious discussion, in a 1966 issue of the *New York Review of Books*.[3] This was a review of J. P. Nettl's two-volume biography, but it more generally engaged (and helped me engage) with Luxemburg's life and meaning. In the late 1960s I ran into members of a somewhat strange sect that was emerging from an organization I was in, Students for a Democratic Society (SDS). The sect was then called the National Caucus of Labor Committees, and although it came to a bad end, at the time its members were extolling Rosa Luxemburg to the skies—so from them I purchased an edition (produced by a mass Trotskyist party in what was then Ceylon, now Sri Lanka) of her 1906 pamphlet, *Mass Strike: The Political Party and the Trade Unions*.[4]

An essential part of my reading and understanding Luxemburg was my own particular context. My father had devoted most of his life to being part of the US labor movement, as a militant union organizer and capable functionary. This was a source of pride for him, and it very much spilled over to me. Yet I sensed that not everything conformed, in practice, to the high ideals that animated him. Some of what Luxemburg had to say seemed to shed light on that.

Similarly, as the volatile 1960s came to an end, the president of the United States escalated the brutal US war against Vietnam with a full-scale invasion of Cambodia. There was a nationwide spontaneous mass upsurge and student strike (complete with numerous university occupations and closures), in which I participated as a "new left" activist in Pittsburgh. I could see some of what Luxemburg wrote about in 1906 exploding all around me, and I learned lessons that could not have been learned otherwise about the pulsating back-and-forth between theory and practice.

Not long after (still in 1970), Pathfinder Press published *Rosa Luxemburg Speaks*, edited by Mary-Alice Waters of the US Socialist Workers Party; it contained most of her pamphlets and articles published in English up to that time. I grabbed and devoured it. Two years later Monthly Review Press published a new translation of Paul Frölich's biography *Rosa Luxemburg*, which I also grabbed and devoured. I was in love, and she has been one of my closest comrades ever since. Over time, I absorbed more deeply perceptions and insights drawn from her work, and when I first began trying to make my own contributions to Marxism, she was part of me.

THE ESSAYS

The first of the items gathered in this volume, "Rosa Luxemburg (1871–1919)," was an entry in the eight-volume *Encyclopedia of Revolution and Protest*, which I helped to edit with the remarkable Manny Ness and others, and which appeared in 2009. It briefly outlines her life and ideas and their context; it also provides a recommended reading list (which includes many of the references cited here).

Ten years earlier, I wrote the second essay, "Revolutionary Mind and Spirit," which first appeared (under the title "A Revolutionary Woman in Mind and Spirit: The Passions of Rosa Luxemburg") in *Against the Current* (no. 80, May–June 1999).

The third essay, "Luxemburg and the German Labor Movement," flows from the fact that the ongoing struggle of the working class to free itself from all forms of oppression and exploitation was central to Luxemburg's life and thought. People all too frequently talk about her "great soul" and her revolutionary-humanistic idealism, while neglecting that she was an integral part of the labor movement; for them the actual working class had become a vague abstraction. I sought to tilt things toward a better balance in presentations at the Conference on Rosa Luxemburg, War and Imperialism in Johannesburg, South Africa, at the Workers Library and Museum, sponsored by the South Africa office of the Rosa Luxemburg Foundation and the Anti-War Coalition in May 2004. Under the title "The Revolutionary Orientation of Rosa Luxemburg," it was published in *Labor Standard* (June 6, 2004).

The fourth item, "Lenin and Luxemburg on Organization," is my first essay on Luxemburg. I wrote it in the 1980s as I was working on my book *Lenin and the Revolutionary Party*. I showed the essay (some of which appears in the Lenin book) to Ernest Mandel, who saw to it that it was published in what was then the theoretical journal of the Fourth International (*International Marxist Review* 2, no. 3, Summer 1987). It was republished in my edited volume, *Rosa Luxemburg: Reflections and Writings.* A more recent essay entitled "Luxemburg and Lenin Through Each Other's Eyes," in my collection *Unfinished Leninism*, discusses other aspects of their relationship.[5]

The fifth essay is the result of the convening of the International Conference on Rosa Luxemburg's Thought and Its Contemporary Value, held March 20–22, 2006, at one of China's most prestigious educational institutions, Wuhan University, under the sponsorship of the similarly prestigious Philosophy School and Institute of Marxist Philosophy. "The Challenge of Revolutionary Democracy" is the presentation I gave at that conference, which first appeared in *International Viewpoint* (September 23, 2006). My report on the conference, "Rosa Luxemburg in the People's Republic of China," was published in *Europe Solidaire Sans Frontières* (Europe: Solidarity without Borders, March 31, 2006; http://www.europe-solidaire.org/spip.php?article4928/). The sixth essay blends politics with creative literature. "Heart of Darkness" discusses imperialism and its implications for the present and future, relating Luxemburg's insights with those of such writers as Joseph Conrad, George Orwell, Herman Melville, and Mark Twain. It was written for a special issue of *New Formations: A Journal of Culture, Theory and Politics* (no. 94, Autumn 2018).

"Celebrating Rosa Luxemburg's Letters" is one of the few writings anywhere crediting Luxemburg's cat Mimi with feline contributions to revolutionary Marxism. It was delivered at an event to celebrate both the launch of the *Complete Works of Rosa Luxemburg* and publication of its preliminary volume, *The Letters of Rosa Luxemburg*.[6] The event—The Life, Letters, and Legacy of Rosa Luxemburg at New York University on March 11, 2011—included several speakers and beautiful readings from the letters by author Deborah Eisenberg (fortunately available online). This was organized by Verso Books staff member Clara Heyworth, a vibrant young woman who was a joy to work with. Four months after the event, in the late evening, Clara was struck and killed by a car operated by a drunken, unlicensed driver. This modest essay is dedicated to her memory.

The eighth item, blending art and politics, is "Comic Book Rosa." It reviews *Red Rosa: A Graphic Biography of Rosa Luxemburg*, by Kate Evans, edited by Paul Buhle, a provocative visual survey of her life and ideas; this review first appeared in the online edition of *Socialist Worker* on November 9, 2015.

The ninth essay, "Rosa Luxemburg for Our Own Time," was a talk given at an International Rosa Luxemburg Conference in Turkey at Bilgi University in Istanbul, November 22–23, 2013, sponsored by the university and by the Rosa Luxemburg Foundation. It contains ideas drawn from many talks given over the years and represents an effort to push through to connect theorizations with practical work.

The tenth piece, which I have entitled "Questions and Reflections," is not an essay at all, but an interview. A version of it appeared in David Muhlmann, *Réconcilier marxism et démocratie*, a book consisting of Muhlmann's own analyses plus interviews with (in addition to me) Daniel Bensaïd, Michael Löwy, Paul Singer, Isabel Loureiro, Toni Negri, Michael Krätke, and Nahiriko Ito.[7] The interview was conducted in English by telephone, and I was very pleased with how it went. Sadly, I am not at all fluent in French, and I had a friend retranslate it back into English for this volume. I then discovered how terribly tricky such translation/retranslation stuff can be. That is especially true when much depends on terminological and political nuance. In parts of the doubly translated interview I seemed to be speaking nonsense, sometimes saying things that are the opposite of what I believe. Some readers may feel that the partially revised and reworded interview presented here still *is* nonsense, but at least it is nonsense that I happen to believe in.

A multiperson debate with Stephen Eric Bronner and others in *New Politics* occasioned the composition of the eleventh essay. Editor Julius Jacobson asked me to participate, resulting in "Why Should We Care What Luxemburg Thought?" (which first appeared in *New Politics* 9, no. 1, Summer 2002). It was reprinted in Jason Schulman, ed., *Rosa Luxemburg: Her Life and Legacy*, which included the entire debate plus three new pieces.[8] The author of one of the new pieces (and consequently one of the book's reviewers) bundled me together with some of the other debaters. According to this, I was "defending a revolutionary councilist tradition that seeks to overthrow the republican state and replace it with a network of direct organs of popular control," whatever that is supposed to mean. That is not my argument at all (as more careful readers will perceive, I hope). In fact, what I wrestle with is a very different question, which Bronner highlighted and which is addressed in other writings here: *In*

*what ways is Rosa Luxemburg relevant to those of us living in a very different
time and place, especially in the absence of the kind of massive and self-conscious
working-class movement that she was part of?*

The final item in this collection was written one century after Rosa
Luxemburg's death. It was solicited by Alan Maass, then editor of *Socialist
Worker* (which ceased publication after the dissolution of the International
Socialist Organization in April 2019), and it appeared under the title "The
Revolutionary Socialism of Rosa Luxemburg" in the print edition of the
January 2019 issue.

CONCLUDING THOUGHTS

I want to conclude with an appeal that we engage with Rosa Luxemburg
in the manner she deserves, and this has several aspects. One involves
opening our minds and hearts to her—and for many of us this is
incredibly easy, given her vibrant sensibilities, her energy, her personal
and intellectual animation and depth, and the very way she talks to us in
her writings.

Another involves trying to understand what she actually said and meant
and did (as opposed to settling for a Rosa simply of our own making). It is
possible to construct one's very own Rosa Luxemburg. I have heard people
describe her essentially as a utopian radical feminist or as a rigidly "Marxist"
antifeminist. I have heard people talk about her (and quite positively) as
if her thinking was compatible with the anarchism of Emma Goldman or
the social-democratic reformism of Eduard Bernstein or the bureaucratic
state capitalism of Deng Xiaoping. She is also very frequently cast in the
role of Lenin's Most Magnificent Enemy in some cosmic morality play.

It is possible to play this with a negative twist. To some on the right—
simply because she is a Marxist, believing in the class struggle and
opposing capitalism—she is a precursor of Joseph Stalin and a herald of
horrific dictatorship. To some on the left, she is criticized as a woolly-
minded "spontaneist" who does not understand the need for organization
in the revolutionary struggle.

Luxemburg was qualitatively different from, and more interesting than,
any of this, and she deserves better from us.

Related to this, she deserves from us an effort to make use of what
she is actually offering us. She was brilliant, insightful, with considerable

knowledge and practical experience. She surely said and wrote things that are worth comprehending, actively considering, and testing out as we try to understand and change the world around us.

No less important than any of this, and very much a part of adhering to the previous recommendations and admonitions, through our engagement with her we must treat her as a person, not as a Revolutionary Goddess. Just because she thinks or says or writes something does not necessarily make that "something" true. It is possible that she could be wrong. Given her humanity, it is inevitable that she would get some things wrong. It has been argued intelligently that there are certain things she got terribly, even disastrously, wrong—and such arguments deserve serious consideration. I should add that, from my own experience, even when I conclude she was wrong about something, it is not the case that she is wrong about every aspect of that "something"—her mind and insights are so good that one can learn from her even when she is partly or largely wrong.

To sum up, she deserves from us that we take her seriously. We owe that to ourselves as well. My hope is that in this book, however imperfectly, I have been able to do all of these things and have helped further the process through which others will do likewise.

1

ROSA LUXEMBURG
(1871–1919)

Rosa Luxemburg was born in a Poland divided under German and Russian domination, and she played a role in the revolutionary movement of each country. Her influence has been global, however, since her contributions place her within the very heart of the Marxist tradition.

Part of a cultured and well-to-do family in Warsaw, Luxemburg was an exceptionally bright child who was encouraged to pursue an education in Poland and then at the University of Zurich in Switzerland, where she received a doctorate in economics with a dissertation titled "The Economic Development of Poland." She became active in the revolutionary socialist movement while still in her teens, soon rising into the leadership circle of the Social-Democratic Party of the Kingdom of Poland, a militant group whose antinationalist orientation caused it to be outpaced by other currents emphasizing the cause of Polish independence.

Luxemburg's working-class internationalism, however, prompted her move to Germany in order to play a more substantial role in the massive and influential Social Democratic Party (SPD) there. Luxemburg soon occupied a place in the revolutionary wing of the socialist movement, gaining considerable respect and also attracting considerable hostility.

QUALITY OF MARXISM

Among Luxemburg's best known early writings are her polemic *Reform or Revolution?* (1899) and her more reflective "Stagnation and Progress of Marxism" (1903), both of which give a sense of the quality of her Marxism.[1] The first involves a debate with a prominent SPD theoretician, Eduard Bernstein. The revolutionary approach of Karl Marx, according to Bernstein, was no longer relevant to modern capitalism and new

German realities; he was convinced that the trade unions and reform efforts within the German parliament, both associated with the practice of the SPD, promised the piecemeal elimination of various oppressive aspects of capitalism and a gradual evolution to socialism. This approach was consistent with the actual practice of the SPD, he argued, not the commitment to the old notion that the working class should take political power in order to inaugurate the socialist transformation. In his view, this was related to a natural tendency in capitalist development for the economy to become socially organized and therefore to evolve in a socialist direction.

Luxemburg sharply challenged this view. She scoffed at Bernstein's method of "weighing minutely the good and bad sides of social reform and social revolution . . . in the same manner in which cinnamon or pepper is weighed out." This method of analysis, in which one could select methods of historical development "out of pleasure from the historical counter of history, just as one chooses hot or cold sausages," constituted the abandonment of "dialectics and . . . the materialist conception of history" that had guided Marx for an inferior method leading in the opposite direction—pushing "the labor movement into bourgeois paths" and "paralyze completely the proletarian class struggle." Following this method, the SPD program would become "not the realization of socialism, but the reform of capitalism." The very nature of capitalism—at the heart of the functioning of the capitalist economy—involved maximizing profits for the capitalist minority through a relentless exploitation of the working-class majority. It is true, she noted, that under capitalism "production takes on a progressively increasing social character," but the capitalist form of this "social character"—including the rise and incredible expansion of powerful economic corporations—would mean that "capitalist antagonisms, capitalist exploitation, the oppression of labor-power, are augmented to the extreme."[2]

Luxemburg insisted that Marx's insight—that "capitalism, as a result of its own inner contradictions, moves toward a point when it will be unbalanced, when it will simply become impossible"—remained as valid as ever. This would cause capitalism's defenders to resist and push back both social reforms and the increasingly "inconvenient" democratic forms that had been conceded in the face of previous revolutionary struggles. She was quite critical of the undemocratic limitations of Germany's parliamentary system—hobbled by the power of monarchy, aristocracy, and big business—and she dismissed Bernstein's notion that this "poultry-yard of bourgeois parliamentarism" could be utilized "to realize the most formidable social transformation of history, the passage from capitalism to socialism." It would become necessary for the workers to push past these limitations, in the direction of genuine "rule by the people" (that is, to political rule by the working class). "In a word, democracy is indispensable not because it renders superfluous the conquest of political power by the proletariat, but because it renders this conquest both necessary and possible."[3]

Arguing that the socialist movement must fight for "the union of the broad popular masses with an aim reaching beyond the existing social order, the union of the daily struggle with the great world transformation" from capitalism to socialism, Luxemburg saw revolutionary Marxism as the most effective means for helping the labor movement to avoid two negative extremes: "abandoning the mass character of the [SPD] or abandoning its final aim [and] falling into bourgeois reformism . . ."[4]

On the other hand, Luxemburg warned that, to a large extent, what passed for "Marxism" in the mass socialist movement was far more limited and dogmatic than the far more complex and nuanced body of thought of Marx ("his detailed and comprehensive analysis of capitalist economy, and . . . his method of historical research with its immeasurable field of application"). She argued that much of this had gone beyond the initial practical needs of the working-class movement, and that "it is not true, as far as the practical struggle is concerned, Marx is out of date, that we have superseded Marx. On the contrary, it is because we have not yet learned to make adequate use of the most important mental weapons in the Marxist arsenal . . . [because the labor movement had not felt] the urgent need of them in the earlier stages of our struggle."[5]

Luxemburg's belief was that developments of the twentieth century would create such an "urgent need," and that rather than allowing the limited "orthodox Marxism" to co-exist with the reformist practice hailed by Bernstein, the SPD and the world socialist movement would need to be revitalized with the more profoundly revolutionary orientation represented by Marx's actual perspectives. At the same time, the spread of the critical Marxist approach (what she termed "the Marxist method of research [being] socialized") would help theorists and activists in the workers' movement to come to grips with the new developments confronting them, with innovative analyses, strategies, and tactics.

ANALYSES OF CAPITALISM AND IMPERIALISM

Applying the dialectical approach to her economic studies, Luxemburg understood capitalism as an expansive system driven by the dynamic of accumulation. Capital in the form of money is invested in capital in the form of raw materials and tools and labor-power, which is transformed— by the squeezing of actual labor out of the labor-power of the workers— into capital in the form of the commodities thereby produced, whose increased value is realized through the sale of the commodities for more money than was originally invested, which is the increased capital out of which the capitalist extracts his profits, only to be driven to invest more capital for the purpose of achieving ever greater capital accumulation.

Luxemburg's analysis of the capital accumulation process involves a complex critique of the second volume of Marx's *Capital*. As part of her resolution of what she considers to be an underdeveloped and incomplete aspect of Marx's analysis of how surplus value is realized, she focuses on the global dynamics of the capitalist system and argues that imperialism is at the heart of capitalist development.

In her classic *The Accumulation of Capital* (1913) she offers an incisive economic analysis of imperialism. There are several distinctive features of Luxemburg's theory of imperialism that sets it off from that of other leading Marxists. She makes a great deal of the co-existence in the world of different cultures, different types of society, and different modes of production (i.e., different economic systems). Historically the dominant form of economy worldwide was the communal hunting and gathering mode of production, which was succeeded in many areas by a more or less communistic agricultural form of economy (which she characterized as a primitive "peasant economy"). This was succeeded in some areas by nonegalitarian societies dominated by militarily powerful elites, constituting modes of production that she labeled "slave economy" and "feudalism." Sometimes coexisting with, sometimes superseding, these modes of production was a "simple commodity production" in which artisans and farmers, for example, would produce commodities for the market in order to trade or sell for the purpose of acquiring other commodities that they might need or want. This simple commodity mode of production is different from the capitalist mode of production, which is driven by the already-described capital accumulation process, overseen by an increasingly wealthy and powerful capitalist minority.

Three features especially differentiate the analysis in *The Accumulation of Capital* from the perspectives of other prominent Marxists.

1. Luxemburg advances a controversial conceptualization of imperialism's relationship to the exploitation of the working class in advanced capitalist countries. Because workers receive less value than they create, they are unable to purchase and consume all that is produced. This underconsumption means that capitalists must expand into noncapitalist areas, seeking markets as well as raw materials and investment opportunities (particularly new sources of labor) outside of the capitalist economic sphere.

2. Another distinctive quality of her conceptualization of imperialism is that it is not restricted to "the highest stage" or "latest stage" of capitalism. Rather, imperialism is something that one finds at the earliest beginnings of capitalism—in the period of what Marx calls "primitive capitalist accumulation"[6]—and which continues nonstop, with increasing and overwhelming reach and velocity, down to the present. Or as she puts it, "capitalism in its full maturity also depends in all respects on non-capitalist strata and social organizations existing side by side with it [and] since the accumulation of capital becomes impossible in all points without non-capitalist surroundings, we cannot gain a true picture of it by assuming the exclusive and absolute domination of the capitalist mode of production."[7]

3. Another special feature of Luxemburg's contribution is her anthropological sensitivity to the impact of capitalist expansion on the rich variety of the world's peoples and cultures. The survey of capitalist expansionism's impact in her *Accumulation of Capital* includes such examples as the destruction of the English peasants and artisans; the destruction of the Native American peoples (the so-called Indians); the enslavement of African peoples by the European powers; the ruination of small farmers in the mid-western and western regions of the United States; the onslaught of

French colonialism in Algeria; the onslaught of British colonialism in India; British incursions into China, with special reference to the Opium Wars; and the onslaught of British colonialism in South Africa (with lengthy reference to the three-way struggle of Black African peoples, the Dutch Boers, and the British).

No less dramatic is Luxemburg's perception of the economic role of militarism in the globalization of the market economy. "Militarism fulfils a quite definite function in the history of capital, accompanying as it does every historical phase of accumulation," she commented, noting that it was decisive in subordinating portions of the world to exploitation by capitalist enterprise. It played an increasingly explosive role in rivalry between competing imperialist powers. More than this, military spending "is in itself a province of accumulation," making the modern state a primary "buyer for the mass of products containing the capitalized surplus value," although in fact, in the form of taxes, "the workers foot the bill."[8]

REVOLUTIONARY STRATEGY AND ORGANIZATION

Luxemburg was profoundly critical of conservative developments in the SPD. An increasingly powerful tendency inside the party and trade union leadership was quietly moving along the reformist path outlined by Bernstein. This path, she prophetically insisted, would not lead gradually to socialism at all, but to the gradual accommodation and subjugation of the socialist movement to the authoritarian proclivities, the brutal realities, and the violent dynamics of the capitalist system.

Luxemburg's revolutionary orientation resonated throughout much of the German labor movement. There were, however, powerful trade union leaders who despised her. They were insulted by her comment, in *The Mass Strike: The Political Party and the Trade Unions* (1906), that trade union struggles can only be like the labor of Sisyphus (rolling the boulder up a hill, only to have capitalist dynamics push the gains back down again) and that only socialism will secure permanent gains for the working class. Although she argued that it is *necessary* for trade unions to wage that struggle in order to defend and improve the workers' conditions in the here-and-now, this did not soften her barbed observation that "the specialization of professional activity as trade-union leaders, as well as the naturally restricted horizon which is bound up with disconnected economic struggles in a peaceful period, leads only too easily, among trade union officials, to bureaucratism and a certain narrowness of outlook."[9]

As Luxemburg explained it, the workings and contradictions of capitalism can sometimes result in what she called a "violent and sudden jerk which disturbs the momentary equilibrium of everyday social life," aggravating "deep-seated, long-suppressed resentment" among workers and other social layers, resulting in an explosive and spontaneous reaction on a mass scale—in the form of strikes spreading through an industry and sometimes involving many, most, or all occupations and workplaces in one or more regions. Such mass strikes can go far beyond economic issues, sometimes involving whole communities in mass demonstrations and street battles, and are the means by which workers seek to "grasp at new political rights and attempt to defend existing ones."[10] Once such strikes begin, there can occur tremendous solidarity, discipline, and effective organization. But they have an elemental quality, which defies any notion of revolutionary blueprints being drawn up in advance.

Luxemburg believed that what she defined as "the most enlightened, most class-conscious vanguard of the proletariat" (among whom she included the SPD in Germany, along with organized socialist parties of other countries) should play an active role not only when such explosions occur, but also beforehand in helping to educate and organize more and more workers in preparation for such developments, which would enable socialist parties to assume leadership of the whole movement. She did not think such upsurges would necessarily result in socialist revolution, but she believed that they would become "the starting point of a feverish work of organization" that would embrace more of the working class, enabling it to fight for reforms in a manner that would help prepare it for the revolutionary struggle: "From the whirlwind and the storm, out of the fire and glow of the mass strike and the street fighting rise again, like Venus from the foam, fresh, young, powerful, buoyant trade unions." Some segments of the working class cannot be unionized through "the form of quiet, systematic, partial trade union struggles," she noted, and her words drive home the point that "a powerful and reckless fighting action of the proletariat, born of a revolutionary situation, must surely react upon the deeper-lying layers and ultimately draw all those into a general economic struggle who, in normal times, stand aside from the daily trade union fight."[11]

Luxemburg taught that in order to remain true to its democratic and socialist principles, and in order to defend the material interests of the workers and the oppressed, the socialist workers' movement, even while fighting for necessary and life-giving partial reforms, would sometimes find itself in uncompromising confrontation with the capitalist power structure. What she and her revolutionary-minded comrades found, however, is that the increasingly bureaucratized structure of their own socialist workers' movement was becoming an obstacle to the internal democracy of the movement. The increasingly bureaucratic-conservative leadership of the trade unions and party more and more sought to contain radicalizing impulses of the working-class membership, to limit the ability of people such as Luxemburg to present a revolutionary socialist perspective, to deflect upsurges in the class struggle into safely moderate channels. She also gave great weight to so-called "extra-parliamentary" social struggles and to a dynamic interplay between existing organizations and spontaneous mass action. She put it this way in her later comments in the wake of Russia's 1917 revolution:

> As bred-in-the-bone disciples of parliamentary cretinism, these German social democrats have sought to apply to revolutions the homemade wisdom of the parliamentary nursery: in order to carry anything, you must first have a majority. The same, they say, applies to the revolution: first let's become a "majority." The true dialectic of revolutions, however, stands this wisdom on its head: not through a majority to revolutionary tactics, but through revolutionary tactics to a majority—that is the way the road runs. Only a party which knows how to lead, that is, to advance things, wins support in stormy times.[12]

For Luxemburg there was a consistency between this revolutionary-democratic strategic perspective and her revolutionary-democratic vision of socialism. Here is how she put it:

> Bourgeois class rule has no need of the political training and education of the entire mass of the people, at least not beyond certain narrow limits. But for the proletarian dictatorship that is the life element, the very air without which it is not able to exist. . . . Only experience is capable of correcting and opening new ways. Only unobstructed, effervescing life falls into a thousand

new forms and improvisations, brings to light creative force, itself
corrects all mistaken attempts. . . . The whole mass of the people
must take part. . . . Socialism in life demands a complete spiritual
transformation in the masses degraded by centuries of class rule.
Social instincts in place of egotistical ones, mass initiative in place
of inertia, idealism which conquers all suffering. . . . The only way to
a rebirth is the school of public life itself, the most unlimited, the
broadest democracy and public opinion.[13]

Although she was fully supportive of the revolutionary example of Lenin,
Trotsky, and the Bolsheviks in their triumphant Russian insurgency of
1917, there were other aspects of the example they were setting to which
she responded more critically.

DEMOCRACY AND FREEDOM

In Luxemburg's view, the socialist movement had proved to be the most
consistent force for democracy in the world. She viewed socialism quite
simply as an expanded, deepened, authentic democracy—genuine rule by
the people in both the political and economic life of society. Her notion
of a workers' state (what has sometimes been called "dictatorship of the
proletariat") had nothing to do with a one-party dictatorship ruling in the
name of the people; rather, it meant what Marx and Engels said in the
Communist Manifesto when they spoke of the working class winning the
battle of democracy, what Lenin meant in *The State and Revolution*, when
he spoke of a thoroughgoing political rule by the working class. This was
in contrast to the authoritarian political forms that began to develop all
too soon in the wake of the 1917 Russian Revolution.

Luxemburg was an early critic of this development, challenging Lenin
and the Bolsheviks—whom she held in high esteem—to pull back from
their expansive justifications for the undemocratic emergency measures
that were adopted in the face of both internal counterrevolutionary assaults
and a global capitalist counteroffensive. "Freedom only for the supporters
of the government, only for the members of one party—however numerous
they may be—is no freedom at all," she insisted. "Freedom is always and
exclusively freedom for the one who thinks differently."[14] She elaborated
in a prophetic warning:

Without general elections, without unrestricted freedom of press and assembly, without a free struggle of opinion, life dies out in every public institution, becomes a mere semblance of life, in which only the bureaucracy remains as the active element. Public life gradually falls asleep, a few dozen party leaders of inexhaustible energy and boundless experience direct and rule. Among them, in reality only a dozen outstanding heads do the leading and an elite of the working class is invited from time to time to meetings where they are to applaud the speeches of the leaders, and to approve proposed resolutions unanimously—at bottom, then, a clique affair—a dictatorship, to be sure, not the dictatorship of the proletariat, however, but only the dictatorship of a handful of politicians.[15]

The best way to help overcome such developments, Luxemburg was convinced, was to spread the revolution to more advanced capitalist countries such as Germany, helping to establish a genuine workers' democracy on an increasingly global scale. Her efforts were tragically unsuccessful, however, and her vision of socialism was overwhelmed by the forces to which she had devoted her life to overcoming. In her classic "The Crisis in the German Social Democracy," also known as "The Junius Pamphlet" (1916), she had written that humanity stood at a crossroads: either moving forward to socialism or a downward slide into barbarism, "either the triumph of imperialism and the destruction of all culture, and, as in ancient Rome, depopulation, desolation, degeneration, a vast cemetery, or the victory of socialism, that is, the conscious struggle of the international proletariat, against its methods, against war."[16]

LIFE AND DEATH

Luxemburg was a theorist, writer, and educator in the socialist movement, teaching at the prestigious school of the SPD, writing articles for its press, and giving innumerable speeches. But she was also an organizer and activist, imprisoned more than once—by Russian authorities in the wake of the 1905 revolutionary upsurge and by German authorities for her uncompromising opposition to World War I. Expelled from the SPD, along with others, she helped to form the Spartakusbund (the Spartacus League, named after the rebellious leader of Roman slaves), which rallied revolutionary socialists (workers as well as intellectuals) to do what the

SPD had ceased to do: oppose war, imperialism, and capitalism. Along with Karl Liebknecht, she was the foremost leader of this current, which also included Franz Mehring, Clara Zetkin, Leo Jogiches, Paul Levi, and others. Shortly before her death, she helped to merge this current with others to found the German Communist Party.

The disastrous conditions created by World War I, and the defeat of Germany, caused the German monarchy to collapse, amid an upwelling of revolutionary sentiment among German workers. Luxemburg was especially critical of secret deals made between SPD moderates and the German military to draw this energy into "safe" channels of a new Weimar Republic that would allow for democratic reforms within a capitalist framework but also allow the old ruling classes to maintain their privileges.

In January 1919, against Luxemburg's warnings, revolutionary euphoria caused some of her comrades, led by Liebknecht, into an ultra-left collision with a better organized, better armed, powerful enemy. In the wake of the revolt's suppression, paramilitary groups (which consisted largely of future Nazis) organized under the name of the Freikorps and—under the pretext of defending the Weimar Republic—systematically rounded up and murdered left-wing "troublemakers." Luxemburg and Liebknecht were among the victims of these death squads.

REFERENCES AND SUGGESTED READINGS

Frölich, P. *Rosa Luxemburg, Her Life and Work.* New York: Monthly Review Press, 1972.

Geras, N. *The Legacy of Rosa Luxemburg.* London: Verso, 1983.

Hudis, P., and K. Anderson, eds. *The Rosa Luxemburg Reader.* New York: Monthly Review Press, 2004.

Le Blanc, P. *From Marx to Gramsci: A Reader in Revolutionary Marxist Politics.* Amherst, NY: Humanity Books, 1996.

———, ed. *Rosa Luxemburg: Reflections and Writings.* Amherst, NY: Humanity Books, 1999.

Luxemburg, R. *The Accumulation of Capital.* New York: Monthly Review Press, 1968.

———. *Rosa Luxemburg Speaks.* Edited by Mary-Alice Waters. New York: Pathfinder Press, 1970.

Nettl, J. P. *Rosa Luxemburg,* 2 vols. London: Oxford University Press, 1966.

2

REVOLUTIONARY MIND AND SPIRIT

In these comments on the spirit and mind of this great revolutionary thinker and activist, I think it makes sense to begin with a focus on her gender. It isn't clear that Rosa Luxemburg herself would be inclined to agree. She had, after all, refused to occupy a "safer" and marginalized position as a women's spokesperson in the socialist movement.

Rosa Luxemburg nonetheless had a vibrant sense of the interpenetration of women's liberation and working-class liberation. In 1902, she wrote that "with the political emancipation of women a strong fresh wind must also blow into [the socialist movement's] political and spiritual life, dispelling the suffocating atmosphere of the present philistine family life which so unmistakably rubs off on our party members too, the workers as well as the leaders."[1]

Despite pioneering work for women's rights by such respected Social Democratic Party leaders as Clara Zetkin and party founder August Bebel, many older male comrades believed that "a woman's place is in the home."

Luxemburg's whole life constituted a conscious and powerful challenge to such sentiments. More than this, there was the painful process of self-definition as she ended her intimate involvement with her first great love, Leo Jogiches.

A master at developing and maintaining revolutionary organizational structures that were especially important for the necessarily clandestine situation of the Polish workers' movement, Jogiches has been well described by Hannah Arendt as "a very remarkable and yet typical figure among the professional revolutionists," combining a strong masculinity with an incisive analytical mind and a deep life commitment to strongly held values and beliefs. There were few men Luxemburg respected, Arendt tells us, "and Jogiches headed a list on which only the names of Lenin and

Franz Mehring could be inscribed with certainty. He definitely was a man of action and passion, and he knew how to do and how to suffer."[2]

Luxemburg's intense, sometimes consuming intimacy with Jogiches lasted amid all the stresses imposed by two strong personalities and by the fluctuating, often tense and difficult conditions of revolutionary struggle from 1892 until 1907. When it finally broke apart—angrily, stormily, and not without some personal destructiveness for them both—Luxemburg nonetheless maintained a comradely working relationship as a political equal with him.

As Raya Dunayevskaya has perceptively suggested, "it was there, *just there*, that something new was emerging." It is highly significant, and appears to set her off from the norm, that (although she continued to have comradely ties, close friendships, and sometimes erotic liaisons) her "further self-development was reaching new heights without leaning on Jogiches" or any other man.[3]

Dunayevskaya stresses: "Luxemburg needed to be free, to be independent, to be whole . . . . Her greatest intellectual accomplishments occurred after the break."[4] It is interesting to note that Luxemburg herself felt that "the character of a woman shows itself not where love begins, but rather where it ends."[5]

I think the question may go deeper than the things already mentioned. To put it bluntly: Did being a woman enable Rosa Luxemburg to develop a Marxist orientation animated by qualities often beyond the reach of her male counterparts?

She was an "outsider" who became a powerful force in the predominantly male milieu in the inner circles of the German, Polish, and Russian left-wing workers' movements, which may have helped her perceive connections less easily visible to others. There were other unusual dimensions of her thought as well.

She proved herself as a brilliant political analyst and a pioneering economic theorist, a fine writer, an inspiring teacher, a powerful speaker, and a revolutionary leader who displayed both courage and insight. But to all of this she brought something different, something special, soaring like an eagle (as Lenin once put it) above most of the others.

There was a sensuousness that was an integral element in how she saw things and expressed them—brushing aside artifice and laughing at posturing, connecting with what was real and dynamic, reaching deep into her own emotional reserves in a way that deeply touched the emotions of others; consistently moving beyond abstractions, nourished by an amazing awareness of the infinite and ever-renewing threads that connect all living things; unashamed of valuing beauty and emotion and nurturing, uncompromisingly honest.

Luxemburg proudly embraced the "scientific socialist" doctrines of Karl Marx, while openly dismissing the vulgar-Marxist notion that "economic development rushes headlong, like an autonomous locomotive on the tracks of history, and that politics, ideology, etc. are content to toddle behind like forsaken, passive freight wagons."[6]

Other mature Marxists had made much the same point—yet this passionate revolutionary consciously fused thought and feeling in an insistent manner that was unusual for the prominent theoreticians who dominated the socialist movement. "Unrelenting revolutionary activity coupled with boundless humanity—that alone is the real life-giving force of socialism," she wrote amid the storms of crashing empires and working-class insurgency in the wake of World War I.[7]

Such expressions (typical of her) set her apart from many of the more "worldly" personalities on the left. Many years before, she had explained to a jaundiced Polish comrade, in regard to the massive Social Democratic Party of Germany, which she had recently joined, that "I do not agree with the view that it is foolish to be an idealist in the German movement." She added: "To begin with, there are idealists here too—above all, a huge number of the most simple agitators from the working masses and furthermore, even in the leadership." But what's more, "the ultimate principle" in all of her revolutionary activity "is to remain true to myself without regard for the surroundings and the others"—thus, "I am and will remain an idealist in the German as well as the Polish movement."[8]

Luxemburg's uncompromising idealism was focused on pushing the German workers' movement to remain true to its original revolutionary perspectives: to win the battle for democracy through an uncompromising struggle by the working class against its oppression (and against all forms of oppression), so that it could finally take state power and bring the economy under the control of the working-class majority.

Considerable lip service was given by the Social Democratic Party to such socialist goals, but "when you look around, the Party looks damn bad—completely headless . . . . No one leads it, no one shoulders the responsibility."[9] The result: a drift toward routinism; a pull toward piling up reforms as a substitute for revolutionary struggle; the rising influence of trade union bureaucracies and of the party's vote-chasing electoral apparatus—in short, policies involving an opportunistic adaptation to capitalism.

She had little patience, however, for the ultra-left elements of "supposed orthodox 'radicalism' . . . attacking each of the opportunist imbecilities and submitting it to a garrulous exegesis . . . [and] who endlessly find it necessary to bring the stray lamb, the Party, back into the safe fold of 'firmness of principles' without realizing that these negative proceedings will not get us ahead even one step."[10]

Instead, as working-class support for the Social Democratic Party shifted from hundreds of thousands to millions of people, "we ourselves must move ahead, develop our tactics, reinforce the revolutionary side of the movement," which she believed would become possible—and effective—in the revolutionary storms that would soon transform "the stagnant waters of the movement" into "a strong fresh current"—which indeed came to pass in the mass strikes and revolutionary upheavals that swept Eastern Europe in 1905–6.[11]

As historian Gary Steenson has commented, "it was her willingness to act . . . that gave legitimacy to her position; unlike others in the [Social Democratic Party of Germany], Rosa Luxemburg was neither an armchair revolutionary nor a firebrand who expected others to carry out the real struggle in the streets."[12]

With the temporary abatement of the revolutionary upsurge, the forces of moderation and opportunism became stronger than ever in the German party.

A cautious trade unionism had become predominant, and trade union leaders indignantly dismissed the mass strike concept with the comment that "the general strike is general nonsense." Rather, as historian John Moses explains, the union leadership "advocated the patient adaptation to existing forces with the ultimate aim of winning piecemeal concessions from both government and management."[13]

This was matched by an increasingly moderate parliamentary strategic orientation, in part because the labor bureaucracy had sought to make the Social Democratic Party—in the satisfied words of trade union head

Karl Legien—into "the representative of the political interests of the trade unions."[14]

In addition, the party apparatus itself, as scholar Richard N. Hunt has noted, had been "created during a long period of social stability and economic expansion, [and] it was hired to run election campaigns, handle finances, disseminate the press, and do everything possible to attract new voters."[15]

Party functionaries were not inclined "to mount barricades or overturn existing society, but only to work within it for the attainment of a socialist [electoral] majority." For this they preferred "a moderate, easy-to-sell program appealing to the widest possible audience," enabling the party to become a sufficiently powerful force in parliament to pass beneficial social legislation.[16]

Even if this strategic course was justified with "orthodox Marxist" rather than "revisionist" phrases, it added up to a reformist orientation, which Luxemburg saw as evolving into an accommodation to an oppressive capitalist status quo.[17]

Yet Luxemburg was convinced that "the masses, and still more the great mass of comrades, in the bottom of their hearts have had enough of this parliamentarism," as she wrote to her like-minded comrade Clara Zetkin in 1907. "I have the feeling that a breath of fresh air in our tactics would be greeted with cries of joy. But still they submit to the heel of the old authorities and, what's more, to the upper strata of opportunist editors, deputies, and trade union leaders."[18]

Economic and political developments were transforming the realities facing the German workers' movement, opening up new opportunities, creating new moods within the working class, but also highlighting inadequacies in the increasingly bureaucratized apparatus of the German Social Democratic Party.

By 1910, Carl Schorske has noted, "the mood of the Social Democratic rank and file waxed stormier as the hopelessness of reform from the top grew more apparent from week to week," and it was Luxemburg "who took the intellectual leadership of the movement to drive on to more radical action."[19]

Yet time was running out. "We are approaching the time when the Party masses will need a leadership that is aggressive, pitiless, and visionary," she commented in 1912, but she noted that "our higher leadership cadres,

the party paper, parliamentary group, as well as our theoretical organ"
threatened to "grow shabbier and shabbier, more cowardly, more besotted
with parliamentary cretinism."[20]

Within two years, her warnings were confirmed more disastrously
than even she had expected, when the bulk of the socialist leadership
led the party into an accommodation with imperialism and militarism—
abandoning the traditional clarion call "workers of all countries unite" in
order to embrace patriotism and support the German war effort in World
War I.

The influence of nationalism and the success of prowar "patriotic"
appeals within much of the working class—used by some Social
Democrats to explain part of their own support for the war effort, and
pointed to by other comrades as a bitter betrayal of the Marxist principles
of working-class internationalism and proletarian revolution—was seen
by Luxemburg from a different perspective.

Her view of the interplay between the masses of the working class and
revolutionary leadership is marked by a striking dynamism:

> There is nothing more mutable than human psychology. The psyche
> of the masses like the eternal sea always carries all the latent
> possibilities: the deathly calm and the roaring storm, the lowest
> cowardice and the wildest heroism. The mass is always that which
> it must be according to the circumstances of the time, and the mass
> is always at the point of becoming something entirely different than
> what it appears to be. A fine captain he would be who would chart his
> course only from the momentary appearance of the water's surface
> and who would not know how to predict a coming storm from the
> signs in the sky or from the depths .... The "disappointment over the
> masses" is always the most shameful testimony for a political leader. A
> leader in the grand style does not adapt his tactics to the momentary
> mood of the masses, but rather to the iron laws of development; he
> holds fast to his tactics in spite of all "disappointments" and, for the
> rest, calmly allows history to bring its work to maturity.[21]

Related to this was the firm belief that when and where the German
socialist movement was strong and effective, the German working class
had learned that "socialism is not only a question of the knife and fork, but
of a cultural movement and a great and proud worldview."[22]

Recalling that Marx and Engels themselves had proclaimed that "the German proletariat has become the heir of classical German philosophy," Luxemburg mused that "since their terrible collapse in the world war, the inheritors look like miserable beggars, eaten alive by vermin." But as she wrote to her friend Franz Mehring, "the iron laws of the historical dialectic . . . will force these beggars to stand up and turn into proud and tough fighters" animated by "the spirit of socialism."[23]

Hardly viewing history as the inexorable movement of impersonal forces bringing about hoped-for revolutionary results, Luxemburg believed in the importance of what people like herself did or failed to do. Revolutionary leadership meant putting forward clear ideas that would help masses of workers as they sought to make sense of the realities of which they were part.

It meant winning people to a revolutionary program—a fighting strategy and practical tactics—that could bring the working class to power. How one advanced this orientation could be decisive in moving forward the class struggle and the revolutionary process.

"Do you know what keeps bothering me now?" she once wrote in an 1898 letter. "I'm not satisfied with the way in which people in the party usually write articles. They are all so conventional, so wooden, so cut and dry." In the opinion of the twenty-seven-year-old revolutionary Marxist, one must do better:

> Our scribblings are usually not lyrics, but whirrings, without color or resonance, like the tone of an engine-wheel. I believe that the cause lies in the fact that when people write, they forget for the most part to dig deeply into themselves and to feel the whole import and truth of what they are writing. I believe that every time, every day, in every article you must live through the thing again, you must feel your way through it, and then fresh words—coming from the heart and going to the heart—would occur to express the old familiar thing. But you get so used to a truth that you rattle off the deepest and greatest things as if they were the "Our Father." I firmly intend, when I write, never to forget to be enthusiastic about what I write and to commune with myself.[24]

By the time she was in her mid-forties, she confessed to an intimate friend that "in theoretical work as in art, I value only the simple, the tranquil and the bold. This is why, for example, the famous first volume of Marx's Capital, with its profuse rococo ornamentation in the Hegelian style, now seems an abomination to me (for which, from the Party standpoint, I must get 5 years' hard labor and 10 years' loss of civil rights)."[25]

She hastened to add that Marx's economic theories were the bedrock of her own theoretical work, but also emphasized that her "more mature" work was in "its form . . . extremely simple, without any accessories, without coquetry or optical illusions, straightforward and reduced to the barest essentials; I would even say 'naked,' like a block of marble."[26]

Delving into theoretical questions—explaining the economic expansionism of imperialism that arose out of the accumulation of capital, which became the title of her 1913 classic—was a creative labor through which "day and night I neither saw nor heard anything as that one problem developed beautifully before my eyes."[27]

The process of thinking—as she slowly paced back and forth, "closely observed by [her cat] Mimi, who lay on the red plush tablecloth, her little paws crossed, her intelligent head following me—and the actual process of writing combined as an experience of trance-like and profound pleasure."[28]

Luxemburg's gifts were hardly restricted to the realm of study and the written word. As a public speaker similar qualities came through.

"An untamed revolutionary force was alive in this frail little woman," an admiring Max Adler later commented. "It was characteristic of her, however, that her intellect never lost control of her temperament, so that the revolutionary fire with which she always spoke was also mingled with cool-headed reflectiveness, and the effect of this fire was not destructive but warming and illuminating."[29] In personal interactions, as well, Luxemburg's student and biographer Paul Frölich tells us, her "large, dark and bright eyes . . . were very expressive, at times searching with a penetrating scrutiny, or thoughtful; at times merry and flashing with excitement. They reflected an ever-alert intellect and an indomitable soul." Her "fine-toned and resonant" voice "could express the finest nuances of meaning," and her slight Polish accent "lent character to her voice and added a special zest to her humor." Frölich tells us that the sensitive revolutionary was by no means full of herself but knew—when with another—that sometimes one must remain silent or listen, and be able to talk "in a natural, down-to-earth, and spirited way" about everyday life. "All this made every private moment with her a special gift."[30]

As the brutalizing World War I dragged on, Luxemburg commented that "although I have never been soft, lately I have grown hard as polished steel, and I will no longer make the smallest concession either in political or personal intercourse." In almost the next breath, she added: "Being a *Mensch* [a person] is the main thing! And that means to be firm, lucid and cheerful. Yes, cheerful despite everything and anything—since whining is the business of the weak. Being a Mensch means happily throwing one's life 'on fate's great scale' if necessary, but, at the same time, enjoying every bright day and every beautiful cloud."[31]

Luxemburg's powerful personality and intellect derived, in large measure, from the fact that she refused to narrow herself (for example, by exclusively focusing on political conflicts), believing that "such one-sidedness also clouds one's political judgment; and, above all, one must live as a full person at all times."[32]

For that matter, although she had more than once suffered from anti-Semitism, she rejected what she viewed as a fixation on "this particular suffering of the Jews," insisting that it was in no way worse than the often murderous oppression of other peoples by European imperialism.

"The poor victims on the rubber plantations in Putumayo, the Negroes in Africa with whose bodies the Europeans play a game of catch, are just as dear to me," Luxemburg wrote to a friend. "Do you remember the words written on the work of the Great General Staff about Trotha's campaign in the Kalahari desert? 'And the death-rattles, the mad cries of those dying of thirst, faded away into the sublime silence of eternity.'" Indignant over the murderous arrogance and smug eloquence of the poetic imperialist, she concluded: "Oh, this 'sublime silence of eternity' in which so many screams have faded away unheard. It rings within me so strongly that I have no special corner of my heart reserved for the [Jewish] ghetto: I am at home wherever in the world there are clouds, birds and human tears."[33]

The violence and inhumanity visited on those victimized by colonial oppression in the "faraway lands" of Asia and Africa became a murderous backdraft which exploded into Europe with the imperialist slaughter of 1914–18. Luxemburg concluded that humanity stood at a crossroads: either forward to socialism or a downward slide into barbarism.

She and her comrades in the newly formed Spartacus League (soon to become the German Communist Party) warned:

The great criminals of this fearful anarchy, of this chaos let loose—the ruling classes—are not able to control their own creation. The beast of capital that conjured up the hell of the world war is not capable of banishing it again, of restoring real order, of insuring bread and work, peace and civilization, and justice and liberty to tortured humanity.

What is being prepared by the ruling classes as peace and justice is only a new work of brutal force from which the hydra of oppression, hatred, and fresh bloody wars raises a thousand heads.[34]

This certainly turned out to be true. The "war to make the world safe for democracy," the "war to end all wars," generated catastrophic aftershocks.[35] Luxemburg herself, and some of her closest comrades, were destroyed by these—which, in turn, helped to undermine the new revolutionary possibilities which she had identified.

It is impossible to measure the loss of this vibrant and magnificent person. The intellectual legacy that she left, however, sheds light not only on the quality of this individual, but also on the times in which she lived, and on the twentieth century as a whole—and perhaps also on the dynamics and possibilities of the twenty-first century.

3

LUXEMBURG AND THE GERMAN
LABOR MOVEMENT

R osa Luxemburg was a brilliant theorist, and her classic *The Accumulation of Capital*—an essential Marxist work on imperialism—continues to be a resource for those who want to understand the world in which we live. But she was committed not only to understanding the world but also to changing it. I want to concentrate here on her thinking about how to do this.

Born into a well-to-do and highly cultured family that would nurture the critical intelligence of this exceptionally bright daughter, Rosa Luxemburg came into the world on March 5, 1871—just before insurgent workers of Paris rose up to establish their heroic and short-lived Commune. Rosa was Polish, not French, but the dual revolution of democratic aspiration and industrial capitalist transformation was generating the rise of the socialist movement on a global scale. She was drawn into the revolutionary movement in Poland before she was fifteen years old. Even as she was completing her formal academic education, which culminated in a doctoral degree in economics at the University of Zurich, she was being trained and tempered in the Marxist underground. Her closest comrades were professional revolutionaries and working-class intellectuals whose lives were an idealistic and passionate blend of revolutionary agitation and organizing, intensive education and analysis, seasoned with debates and polemics, sometimes punctuated by strikes or insurrections, and often laced with prison and martyrdom.[1]

Central to Rosa Luxemburg's strategic orientation for achieving global justice was the commitment to the liberation struggles of the working-class majority. Those whose lives and labor keep society running are the ones who should run society. It is the great majority of the people who must shape the future. "Socialism cannot be made and will not be made by command, not even by the best and most capable Socialist government," she insisted. "It must be made by the masses, through every proletarian individual."[2]

When we try to look at the labor movement to which Rosa Luxemburg belonged, we are at a serious disadvantage. We tend to superimpose our own experience, or our lack of experience blended with various abstract notions, over the living reality of the German workers' movement in which she became involved more than a century ago. There are relatively few studies that try to give a real sense of that movement, and there are very few attempts to connect such things with the biography and ideas of Rosa Luxemburg. In my comments here I want to use one of those rare studies—Mary Nolan's *Social Democracy and Society: Working-Class Radicalism in Dusseldorf, 1890–1920*. And I will make special reference to one of the local working-class activists described in that study, Peter Berten, who was in his mid-twenties when Luxemburg burst on the scene of left-wing German politics in the late 1890s, and in his mid-forties when she was killed by right-wing death squads in 1919.[3]

Luxemburg's views on the labor movement corresponded to those of Karl Marx. She embraced (as did most German Social Democrats) the orientation presented in the *Communist Manifesto*: that the workers should struggle for various reforms to expand democratic rights and improve immediate economic and social conditions, that they should build increasingly effective and inclusive trade unions to secure better working conditions and higher living standards, that they should build their own working-class political party. She accepted Marx's view that the workers' party should struggle to "win the battle for democracy"—winning political power in order to make "despotic inroads" into the capitalist economy for the purpose of bringing about the socialist reconstruction of society. And like Marx, Luxemburg believed that the defenders of the old social order would not permit a peaceful and gradual transition to socialism, that they would unleash violence (perhaps sooner rather than later) to preserve their privileges, and they would have to be overcome through the revolutionary struggle of the workers and their allies.[4]

The specifics of Luxemburg's political orientation assumed the existence of a mass working-class movement that included but went beyond trade unions. There was a vibrant labor press, a network of cooperatives, a political party, and a growing array of cultural institutions.

Peter Berten had completed elementary school and then learned cabinetmaking from his father. For much of his young adulthood, he was an itinerant journeyman moving from job to job in various cities in the Lower Rhine, and soon he became a militant of the woodworkers union. After participating in "lively political discussions at union meetings" over a period of a few years, he joined the Social Democratic Party (SPD) of Germany, and the young worker proved to be a capable and dedicated organizer and agitator for the socialist cause. By 1904, Berten was a central leader of the SPD in Dusseldorf, sometimes serving as the organization's paid secretary, and in 1908 he became the editor of the local newspaper of the Dusseldorf socialists, the *Volkszeitung*, which had a subscription base of 6,000.[5]

In this period trade union membership in Dusseldorf rose from 5,400 in 1903 to almost 25,000 in 1912, with SPD membership rising from 950 to more than 7,000 in the same years, about 98 percent of whom were working class. The SPD vote in Dusseldorf rose from 20,000 in 1903 to more than 42,000 in 1912—just under 50 percent of all Dusseldorf's votes. In 1909 a Volkshaus (People's House, a political and cultural center) was opened by the local SPD, "a home where workers are master," Peter Berten wrote proudly, "and not dependent on the goodwill of speculating parasites . . . a home where they can raise themselves above the misery of daily life, if only for a few hours." In addition to trade unions and the political party, more than 2,000 workers participated in a consumer cooperative, and more than 8,000 each year used the services of legal and social service advisors offered by the Dusseldorf workers' movement. Hundreds participated in workers' education courses ("to expand people's knowledge in the class struggle," as one SPD militant emphasized), dealing with such topics as history, economics, and Marxism. Sometimes thousands each year attended SPD forums on important issues facing the working class, and public protests rallying workers—according to SPD flyers—"to do everything possible to improve the condition of the working class and eliminate capitalism."[6]

Dusseldorf was not unique in urban and industrial sectors of Germany, and it reflected the context in which Luxemburg functioned. Her ideas resonated among many who were part of this labor movement in such places. It is worth emphasizing what is hard for many of us in the United States to remember: The labor movement is much more than the unions. Twenty percent of Dusseldorf workers were in unions, but the ratio of union members to party members shifted from 13 trade unionists for every 1 party member in 1901, to just 5 to 1 by 1907, and 3 to 1 in 1912. Even so, SPD leaders like Berten complained that too many workers remained "just trade unionists."[7]

An aspect of this dilemma was discussed by Luxemburg in 1904 in the following manner:

> The international movement of the proletariat toward its complete emancipation is a process peculiar in the following respect. For the first time in the history of civilization, the people are expressing their will consciously and in opposition to all ruling classes. But this can only be satisfied beyond the limits of the existing system.
>
> Now the mass can only acquire and strengthen this will in the course of the day-to-day struggle against the existing social order— that is, within the limits of capitalist society.
>
> On the one hand, we have the mass; on the other, its historic goal, located outside of existing society. On one hand, we have the day-to-day struggle; on the other, the social revolution. Such are the terms of the dialectical contradiction through which the socialist movement makes its way.
>
> It follows that this movement can best advance by tacking betwixt and between the two dangers by which it is constantly being threatened. One is the loss of its mass character; the other, the abandonment of its goal. One is the danger of sinking back into the condition of a sect; the other, the danger of becoming a movement of bourgeois social reform.[8]

That dilemma relates to a crisis that developed in the German SPD. A strong tendency developed among the national trade union leadership—members of the SPD who were leading relatively strong union organizations, the majority of whose members were not SPD members, organizations whose primary goal was to secure higher wages and better working conditions within the context of the capitalist economy. These trade union leaders wanted to bring the SPD under the control of the unions, to prevent revolutionary-minded socialists from pushing the unions in a more radical direction, and instead getting the SPD to advance the moderate trade union agenda. A layer of the SPD functionaries wanted to go in this moderate direction, which they hoped would help the party accumulate votes of nonradical (and to some extent non-working-class) layers of the population.[9]

The tension between revolutionaries and reformists cropped up over and over, with greater intensity—for example, in 1908 around courses that Luxemburg and others were teaching at the recently established Central Party School in Berlin. Paul Frölich tells us that the more than 200 students who had attended the school came from

> a colorful variety of backgrounds: next to raw youngsters who had only a smattering of socialism, but had distinguished themselves in one way or another in their work for the party, there were old and experienced party workers. They represented a very wide variety of occupations: mechanics, carpenters, decorators, miners, party secretaries, trade unionists, housewives, intellectuals. Most of them had derived their knowledge of socialism only from agitational pamphlets, and were not used to systematic thought.[10]

Peter Nettl records that her students responded to Luxemburg's classes with enthusiasm: "She was a natural and enthusiastic teacher, clarifying the most complicated philosophical issues of Marxism with lively similes and illustrations, making the subject not only real but important."[11]

Those who feared that the wrong kind of workers' education was being conducted at the school demanded that more practical matters take the place of revolutionary abstractions. "Do the masses have to know the theory of value? Do the masses need to know what the materialist theory of history is?" asked Kurt Eisner, who answered his own question with the comment that such stuff has no direct value and can even be harmful for working-class activists, concluding: "Theory frequently has the actual effect of killing the power to come to conclusions and to take action."[12] Luxemburg's retort drew enthusiastic applause at the 1908 Party Congress:

> They think the materialist conception of history, as they understand it, has on them the effect of crippling their ability to act and they therefore think that theory should not be taught at the Party School, but hard facts, the hard facts of life. They haven't the faintest idea

that the proletariat knows the hard facts from its everyday life, the proletariat knows the "hard facts" better than Eisner. What the masses lack is general enlightenment, the theory which gives us the possibility of systematizing the hard facts and forging them into a deadly weapon to use against our opponents.[13]

Peter Berten was a student at the Berlin Party School in 1906, and the classes he took with Luxemburg taught him that "one cannot talk of an automatic development from a capitalist economy to a socialist one. Capitalism lays the basis for a socialist society but the working class must bring it about." Berten's views—as a leader of the SPD in Dusseldorf, and as the editor of the *Volkszeitung*—closely corresponded to the outlook of Luxemburg. He denounced those who were trying, as he put it, to turn the SPD into "a bourgeois radical reform party," insisting that "we have no cause to give up our principles and our tactics. The capitalist system with its injuries cannot be eliminated by concessions to the ruling class and its government." He explained that the SPD was radical in the Lower Rhine, and reformist revisionism could not secure a foothold there, "because the economic and political pressures that bear down on the workers in our region are so strong. Through them the masses are forged together and learn class consciousness and revolutionary thinking." Yet there were fluctuations in working-class consciousness. In 1913, after SPD electoral victories in Dusseldorf, he was warning that "some of our comrades seem to be of the opinion that since we won the Reichstag election everything has been achieved... Most believe that they have fulfilled their responsibilities if they pay their dues and attend an occasional meeting." But the combination of seeking petty reforms while passively waiting for the revolution, Berten insisted, "cannot possibly inspire and sweep along the masses. Only great goals can waken enthusiasm and a willingness to sacrifice."[14]

In Berten's opinion, "Only a revolutionary tactic, which always builds on the reality of class conflict and appeals to the elemental power of the masses, can waken the energy, activism, and enthusiasm of the exploited proletariat." He emphasized in the *Volkszeitung* that "the mass strike is the method of struggle which is most suited to the social position of the proletariat." In his opinion, "What the proletariat possesses, in addition to its chains, is the power that does not disappear through struggle.

Rather it grows until it suffices to break the chains." Mary Nolan reports that "Berten and several other functionaries were the most vociferous proponents of the mass strike, but their ideas found a sympathetic echo among comrades locally and regionally."[15]

As Luxemburg explained it, the workings and contradictions of capitalism can sometimes result in what she called a "violent and sudden jerk which disturbs the momentary equilibrium of everyday social life," aggravating "deep-seated, long-suppressed resentment" among workers and other social layers, resulting in an explosive and spontaneous reaction on a mass scale—in the form of strikes spreading through an industry and sometimes involving many, most, or all occupations and workplaces in one or more regions. Such mass strikes can go far beyond economic issues, sometimes involving whole communities in mass demonstrations and street battles, and are the means by which workers seek to "grasp at new political rights and attempt to defend existing ones." Once such strikes begin, tremendous solidarity, discipline, and effective organization can occur. But they have an elemental quality that defies any notion of revolutionary blueprints being drawn up in advance.

Luxemburg believed that Social Democrats (whom she defined as "the most enlightened, most class-conscious vanguard of the proletariat") should play an active role not only when such explosions occur, but also beforehand in helping to educate and organize more and more workers in preparation for such developments, which would enable Social Democrats to assume leadership of the whole movement. She by no means believed that such upsurges would necessarily result in socialist revolution. But neither did she believe that they would wreck labor organizations. Rather, in her words, they became "the starting point of a feverish work of organization." While labor and socialist bureaucrats might "fear that the organizations will be shattered in a revolutionary whirlwind like rare porcelain," Luxemburg's observations of actual mass strikes during 1905–6 in Eastern Europe showed that the opposite is the case: "From the whirlwind and the storm, out of the fire and glow of the mass strike and the street fighting rise again, like Venus from the foam, fresh, young, powerful, buoyant trade unions." Some segments of the working class cannot be unionized through "the form of quiet, systematic, partial trade union struggles," she noted, and her words drive home the point that "a powerful and reckless fighting action of the proletariat, born of a revolutionary situation, must surely react upon the deeper-lying layers and ultimately draw all those into a general economic struggle who, in normal times, stand aside from the daily trade union fight."[16]

Luxemburg's revolutionary orientation resonated throughout much of the German labor movement. There were, however, powerful trade union leaders who despised her. They were insulted by her comment that trade union struggles can only be like the labor of Sisyphus (rolling the boulder up a hill, only to have capitalist dynamics push the gains back down again), and that only socialism will secure permanent gains for the working class. Of course, she added that it is *necessary* for trade unions to wage that struggle in order to defend and improve the workers' conditions in the here and now. But this did not make up for her barbed observation that "the specialization of professional activity as trade-union leaders, as well as the naturally restricted horizon which is bound up with disconnected economic struggles in a peaceful period, leads only too easily, among trade union officials, to bureaucratism and a certain narrowness of outlook." She was specific: first, there was "an overvaluation of the [trade union] organization, which from a means has gradually been changed into an end in itself, a precious thing, to which the interests of the struggles should be subordinated," and second, "the trade union leaders, constantly absorbed in the economic guerrilla war whose plausible task it is to make the workers place the highest value on the smallest economic achievement, every increase in wages and shortening of the working day, gradually lose the power of seeing the larger connections and taking a survey of the whole position" facing the working class.[17]

But other trade unionists, a left-wing dissident current represented by Peter Berten and others, appreciated her approach to struggling for reforms (relevant to workplace struggles no less than to parliamentary struggles)—the notion that an uncompromising militancy will gain more than an allegedly "practical-minded" moderation. If one wants a shorter work day, for example, and one hears that the bourgeois politicians (or managerial negotiators) are prepared to favor a ten-hour workday but not an eight-hour workday, one should not offer to form an alliance with them in favor of a ten-hour day. One should instead engage in a militant struggle for the eight-hour day as the best means for pressuring them into actually coming up with their ten-hour compromise. This also builds a class-conscious militancy necessary for future struggles.

This orientation comes through even in the way that Luxemburg talks about May Day in 1913. She said: "The brilliant basic idea of May Day is the autonomous, immediate stepping forward of the proletarian masses, the political mass action of the millions of workers who otherwise are atomized by the barriers of the state in the day-to-day parliamentary affairs, who mostly can give expression of their own will only through the ballot, through the election of their representatives." Noting the rising tide of imperialist exploitation and violence, she concluded that "the more the idea of May Day, the idea of resolute mass actions as a manifestation of international unity, and as a means of struggle for peace and for socialism, takes root in the strongest troops of the International, the German working class, the greater is our guarantee that out of the world war which, sooner or later, is unavoidable, will come forth a definite and victorious struggle between the world of labor and of capital."[18]

Despite considerable lip service given to Marxist theory and socialist goals, the German SPD "looks damn bad—completely headless...No one leads it, no one shoulders responsibility," as she put it. Instead there was organizational routinism, there was a focus on winning more elections to put more socialist politicians into parliament where they maneuvered and bargained for limited reforms, and there was the growing influence of a powerful trade union leadership focused on winning piecemeal concessions within the existing social order. Such things tended to remove the masses of workers as an active factor in the struggle for a better future, keeping them under "the heel [as she put it] of the old authorities and, what's more, to the upper strata of opportunist [socialist] editors, [parliamentary] deputies, and trade union leaders."[19]

In the following year, Luxemburg and her revolutionary comrades found themselves trapped in the left wing of a bureaucratized mass party which, when World War I erupted in 1914, supported the brutalizing imperialist war effort instead of organizing working-class resistance. More than this, its leaders looked with relief upon the imprisonment of Rosa Luxemburg for antiwar activity. In the aftermath of the war, as the working-class radicalization foreseen by Luxemburg gathered momentum, the SPD bureaucracy was able to divert much of the proletarian militancy into "safe" channels. Luxemburg and the most committed revolutionaries were first blocked and then expelled, left without an adequate revolutionary instrument of their own. Amid the rising proletarian ferment and counterrevolutionary violence of late 1918 and early 1919, they were forced to begin rebuilding an organization.

Thanks to the working-class and peasant upsurge in their own country and to years of serious organizational development, Lenin and the Bolsheviks had succeeded in 1917 in establishing a revolutionary workers' government in Russia and appealed for the spread of revolutions throughout Europe, and beyond Europe, but in highly industrialized Germany most of all. Increasing numbers of German workers and war-weary soldiers responded with enthusiasm (for that matter, so did Rosa Luxemburg, who soon was released from prison). This coincided with the collapse of the German war effort and the collapse of the monarchy. It seemed that Germany was on the verge of socialist revolution, but the only substantial organizational expression of socialism in the country was the SPD, which by now was in the hands of the worst of opportunistic bureaucrats who were far more hostile to working-class revolution than to their own landed aristocrats and big-business interests. The result was a compact between the party leadership and the German economic elite, also involving the top levels of the old governmental and military apparatus, to preserve as much of the old social order as possible, masked for a short while with socialist and democratic rhetoric.

In order to win the radicalized masses to a genuinely revolutionary socialist alternative, Luxemburg and others formed the Spartakusbund (the Spartacus League, named after the leader of the great slave revolt that shook the Roman empire), which was not strong enough to lead the workers to a revolutionary victory. At the same time, it is important not to underrate the Spartakusbund. Historian William Pelz argues that "by war's end, Spartacus had grown into an organization of thousands with influence in numerous working class areas."[20] Since Pelz has inquired more carefully than most into the nature and dimensions of this movement that Luxemburg led, it is worth considering more of what he has to say in his fine study, *The Spartakusbund and the German Working Class Movement 1914–1919*:

> Struggling underground, the Spartakusbund was able to grow, propagate its ideas and develop linkages with like-minded revolutionary groups and individuals, based heavily in urban industrial areas. Thus, Luxemburg, [Karl] Liebknecht and the other

Spartakusbund leaders directed what was the heart of a growing revolutionary workers movement. Young, active and concentrated in the most modern vital sections of the economy, Spartakusbund members were to prove the revolutionary voice within the ideological vacuum [which the bureaucratized leadership of the German] Social Democracy labored to maintain.[21]

This suggests that if Luxemburg, Liebknecht, and other key Spartacus leaders had not met their deaths in 1919, then around them a powerful, self-confident, increasingly experienced leadership core would have crystallized to lead a growing German Communist Party to victory in, say, 1920 or 1923, when genuine revolutionary possibilities emerged. This would have rescued the Russian Revolution from the isolation that would soon generate Stalinism, at the same time preventing the possibility of the rise of Hitlerism in Germany.

From the standpoint of those determined to preserve the old social order, Rosa Luxemburg could not be allowed to live. The fact that she was a woman, and that her life had included—on her own terms—sensual love and revolutionary activity, made her a special target. The cultural and political reactionaries of her time were fixated on the sexuality and political subversion represented by this "Jewish slut" who was the repulsive "bloody Rosa," someone fit to be murdered in the so-called "Spartacus days" of January 1919, when—against Luxemburg's warnings—revolutionary euphoria led her comrades into an ultra-left collision with a better organized, better armed, powerful enemy that had been waiting for an opportunity to unleash the death squads of the so-called *Freikorps*.

But Luxemburg's vibrant, passionate life and intelligence are with us still in her writings, which continue to have an amazing relevance to the realities that we face today. I think this comrade would want us to give serious thought to the question of what we can do to help change the world to a place in which the free development of each person would be the condition for the development of all. This conference—in which we are collectively seeking to learn the lessons of Luxemburg's ideas and activities, and to apply them to our own time—not only does honor to this wonderful revolutionary, but also (with luck and hard work) can help direct our attention and energies into a hopeful future.

4

LUXEMBURG AND LENIN ON REVOLUTIONARY ORGANIZATION

Among the greatest representatives of the revolutionary Marxist movement in the twentieth century are Rosa Luxemburg and Vladimir Ilyich Lenin. The foremost leader of Russian socialism's left wing, Lenin forged a Bolshevik (majority) faction of the Russian Social Democratic Labor Party (RSDLP) in 1903 which, by 1912, separated to form a distinctly revolutionary workers' party that proved itself by leading the world's first socialist revolution five years later. Luxemburg was in the same period a central leader in the left wing of both the Polish and German socialist movements. Associated throughout her revolutionary career with the Social Democracy of the Kingdom of Poland and Lithuania (SDKPiL) and, in exile from her native Poland, a brilliant light in the massive German Social Democratic Party (SPD), she was the most prominent critic of the theoretical revisionism and practical reformism that were eating away at the integrity of the German workers' movement. Like Lenin, she was a perceptive analyst of imperialism and an uncompromising opponent of World War I. Shortly before she and Karl Liebknecht were murdered during the abortive uprising of 1919, Luxemburg was a founder of the German Communist Party.[1]

Yet much of the attention on Luxemburg in later years has been focused on her 1904 critique of Lenin's ideas on the question of revolutionary organization. Standard interpretations of Luxemburg's critique have her "demonstrate the bureaucratic tendencies inherent in Lenin's conception, speaking of the inevitable strangling of individual initiative in such an organization." This is the interpretation of the former German Communist Franz Borkenau in his anticommunist classic *World Communism* (1938): "Where Lenin, instead of the belief in the proletarian revolution, had put his hopes in a centralized group under his leadership." Borkenau explained: "Rosa Luxemburg almost alone continued to believe in the proletariat . . . The masses must not be ordered about by an 'infallible' central committee. They must learn from their own experience, their own mistakes. Revolution must be the result of their increasing political understanding. She believed, in short, in the spontaneity of the proletarian masses."[2]

This interpretation has found an echo across the political spectrum—among Cold War anticommunist crusaders, among moderate reformist socialists, and even among many who consider themselves revolutionary opponents of capitalism. But it's a myth that obscures the realities of Lenin's politics as well as Luxemburg's. It even blurs the genuine insights that can be found in her critique of Lenin's ideas. Only if we clear away the deadwood of distortion and romanticization can we hope to understand these two revolutionaries, particularly their ideas on the vital question of how revolutionaries should organize themselves in order to be effective in advancing the socialist cause.

LUXEMBURG AND THE POLISH MOVEMENT

The standard generalizations about Luxemburg's opposition to organizational centralism are at once thrown into question if—unlike most commentators—we focus our attention on the role she played in the Polish revolutionary movement, particularly from 1903 to 1913. In Poland, unlike Germany (but like Russia), revolutionaries were compelled to operate in underground conditions. The Polish organization in which she was involved was hardly "Luxemburgist" in the libertarian way that the term is commonly understood. "The Social Democracy of Poland and Lithuania, which she led, was, if anything, far more highly centralized and far more merciless toward those in its ranks who deviated from the party's line, than was the Bolshevik party under Lenin," wrote Max Shachtman in 1938.[3] The knowledgeable ex-anarchist Max Nomad put it more strongly: "And she was also hated by some prominent members of her own Polish Marxist Party whom she mercilessly expelled from the ranks of the organization when they dared to dissent from her views—even though it was known that the dissenters had behind them the majority of the underground membership."[4] More recently, the prominent Belgian

Trotskyist Ernest Mandel commented: "In fact, while criticizing Lenin, Rosa was busy building a centralized (one could say: overcentralized) illegal party in Poland, and conducting faction fights against minorities at least in the same (if not more) 'harsh' manner as Lenin. This is often forgotten in the analysis of the Lenin–Luxemburg controversy on organization, and merits closer attention."[5]

One account of the events alluded to in these judgments has been offered in Peter Nettl's biography *Rosa Luxemburg*. Nettl argued that "Rosa Luxemburg was herself not directly involved," in fact "had nothing to do with" and "disapproved of" the harsh organizational measures for which, according to Nettl, her close comrade Leo Jogiches was primarily responsible.[6]

A more recent study, however, makes it difficult to accept Nettl's interpretation. Jogiches (whose party name was Tyszka) was certainly a central leader in the SDKPiL, but Robert Blobaum has documented that "while Tyszka's claims to political hegemony in the SDKPiL are both undeniable and well-documented, one must be able to distinguish between pretense and fact. The truth of the matter is that Tyszka lacked the political base among the party rank and file necessary to the realization of his ambitions."[7] The central organizational figure was Felix Dzierzhinski, a sincere and dedicated revolutionist whose talents were ultimately to result in his becoming, after the Bolshevik Revolution, the first head of the Soviet republic's secret police, the Cheka. But in the years before that he played a role aptly described in this manner: "As the inspiration behind a constantly evolving organizational apparatus, and as the dominant figure in the executive institutions of the SDKPiL, Dzierzhinski translated the ideas of Luxemburg—edited as they were by Tyszka—into more easily digestible forms of political action."[8] A member of the oppositional faction bitterly commented in 1904 that "the triumvirate of Tyszka, Luxemburg, and Dzierzhinski does what it wants without coming to an agreement with the rest of the members."[9]

Dzierzhinski was determined to forge, in his words, "a new type of organization with no rights but to work, to carry out the instructions of the Foreign Committee (in which Luxemburg's perspectives predominated), to educate itself, to distribute literature, etc. This section shall have no voice at all or any right of representation in the party; its aim is simply to become Social Democratic and to be at the beck and call of the Foreign

Committee."[10] This organizational perspective, justified as a necessary expedient due to Poland's repressive environment, was used to ensure the triumph of the political orientation of "the Luxemburg group" in the SDKPiL. "In assuring the victory of Luxemburg and Tyszka over their émigré opponents," notes Blobaum, "Dzierzhinski had introduced fundamental organizational innovations that were to transform the appearance of the party. By placing himself at the head of party institutions—in the Foreign Committee, in the Main Directorate, and on the editorial board of *Czerwony sztander*—Dzierzhinski concentrated considerable power in his own hands which served to centralize the organization as a whole."[11] Blobaum indicates that all of this had "Luxemburg's blessing" and that she "realized her faction's debt to Dzierzhinski and heaped praise upon his work in a congratulatory letter."[12]

Blobaum argues persuasively that Dzierzhinski was not interested in power for its own sake and was, in fact, committed to a collective leadership with Luxemburg and Jogiches.[13] Channeling his creative energy into tireless organizational work, his goal was to translate the political *Weltanschauung* of "Luxemburgism"—identified by Blobaum as "the emphasis on maximalist demands, exclusiveness in relation to non-proletarian segments of the population, inflexible opposition to the goal of Polish independence under any circumstances, the territorial as opposed to the national character of party work"—into action, bringing it to life through cohesive organization.[14] Blobaum stresses that he was "a Polish revolutionary of the 'internationalist' wing, a true believer of the ideology of Marxism as interpreted by Rosa Luxemburg; significantly, it was her portrait that years later stared at him from a wall of his office at the Lubianka (Cheka headquarters) in Moscow."[15]

Nor can we simply assume that Luxemburg was so immersed in other matters that she was completely ignorant of Dzierzhinski's mode of operation. In 1905 she had an opportunity to get into Poland and Russia where the two revolutionary leaders worked closely and harmoniously.[16] In the period after the defeat of the 1905 revolution, Dzierzhinski, not inclined to tolerate organized opposition to the authority of the SDKPiL's central leadership, "was prepared to employ all means at his disposal to eliminate such opposition."[17] This resulted, in 1911–12, in a split in which Luxemburg played a significant role. One aspect of it was "the Radek case," which involved an effort to expel the dissident Karl Radek not only from the Polish socialist movement but also from the German movement. Luxemburg became deeply involved in this sad and dubious effort.[18]

It is worth noting that Lenin, although an "outsider," himself sympathized with the politics and organizational rights of the dissidents during this affair.

THE IMMEDIATE CONTEXT OF LUXEMBURG'S CRITIQUE

The fact remains, however, that Luxemburg's primary field of operation was within the German SPD. And her 1904 polemic "Organizational Questions of Russian Social Democracy" is more than simply a critique of Lenin's *One Step Forward, Two Steps Back*. Appearing in the German Marxist theoretical magazine *Neue Zeit*, it was introduced with the following editorial comment: "The present work deals with Russian conditions, but the organizational questions with which it deals are also important for the German Social Democracy. This is true not only because of the great international significance which our Russian brother party has achieved, but also because similar questions of organization presently occupy our own party."[19]

If we fail to recognize the significance of Luxemburg's critique for the German context, we will not be able to understand what she was saying. The profound difference between German and Russian realities has been cogently described by Max Shachtman:

> The "professional revolutionists" whom Luxemburg encountered in Germany were not, as in Russia, the radical instruments, for gathering together loose and scattered local organizations, uniting them into one national party imbued with a firm Marxist ideology and freed from the opportunistic conceptions of pure-and-simple trade unionism. Quite the contrary. In Germany, the "professionals" were careerists, the conservative trade-union bureaucrats, the lords of the ossifying party machine, the reformist parliamentarians, the whole crew who finally succeeded in disemboweling the movement... The "centralism" of Lenin forged a party that proved able to lead the Russian masses to victorious revolution, the "centralism" that Luxemburg saw growing in the German social democracy became

a conservative force and ended in a series of catastrophes for the proletariat.[20]

It is also worth noting that while, in this period, Lenin tended to idealize the German SPD as a model (even as he unconsciously diverged from it) because from afar it still seemed a bulwark of Marxist orthodoxy, Luxemburg was already poignantly aware of its deficiencies (even as she was unable fully to transcend them).

Luxemburg's article has a relevance transcending the German context. The very way in which she frames the problem has had a universal resonance down to our own times:

> On the one hand, we have the mass; on the other, its historic goal, located outside of existing society. On the one hand we have the day-to-day struggle; on the other, the social revolution. Such are the terms of the dialectical contradiction through which the socialist movement makes it[s] way.
>
> It follows that this movement can best advance by tacking betwixt and between the two dangers by which it is constantly being threatened. One is the loss of its mass character, the other, the abandonment of its goal. One is the danger of sinking back into the condition of a sect; the other, the danger of becoming a movement of bourgeois social reform.[21]

Luxemburg goes on to criticize Lenin for an "overanxious desire to establish the guardianship of an omniscient and omnipotent Central Committee" in order to protect the Russian workers' movement from opportunism. She argues that "opportunism appears to be a product of an inevitable phase of the historic development of the labor movement," and that it "can be overcome only by the movement itself—certainly with the aid of Marxist theory, but only after the dangers in question have taken tangible form in practice."[22] Compressed into this point is a complex argument that is far richer than such interpreters as Franz Borkenau imply.

The fact remains that the entire argument is advanced as a polemic against Lenin's views. In 1904 Luxemburg did not fully grasp what those views were. In part this was because she, like most well-read Marxists outside of Russia, was influenced by what Lenin's Menshevik opponents (who included most of the best-known Russian Marxists: Plekhanov,

Axelrod, Zasulich, Deutsch, Martov, Potresov, Trotsky, and others) were asserting. In order to better evaluate Luxemburg's critique, we need to examine the circumstances under which the split in the Russian movement took place.

THE RUSSIAN REALITIES

At the Second Congress of the RSDLP in 1903, which resulted in the Bolshevik/Menshevik split, Lenin did not intend to enunciate some "Leninist" doctrine about "a party of a new type." The term Leninism at this time was nothing more than a factional epithet hurled at Lenin and his co-thinkers, who saw themselves, simply, as being the most consistent defenders of the traditional party perspective held in common by Marxists throughout Russia and the world. Even Pavel Axelrod, a veteran socialist on the Menshevik side of the split, believed that there were "no clear, defined differences concerning either principles or tactics" and that on the organizational questions there were no principled differences regarding "centralism, or democracy, autonomy, etc." Rather there were differing opinions regarding the "application or execution of organizational principles . . . (which) we have all accepted."[23]

With the passage of time, far-reaching political differences between the Bolsheviks and Mensheviks *did* become evident, but Lenin perceived this only after he wrote his 1904 discussion of the split, *One Step Forward, Two Steps Back*. The sources of the split were tangled and complex.

Political ideas are held by, and political organizations are composed of, human beings. We cannot afford to lose sight of the interplay between political principles and human dynamics as we attempt to grasp the vibrant reality of an organization's life and development. The 1903 congress of the RSDLP is a classic illustration.

"We all knew each other," wrote Lenin's companion Nadezhda Krupskaya, "not only as Party workers, but in intimate personal life. It was all a tangle of personal sympathies and antipathies. The atmosphere grew tenser as the time for voting approached."[24] Despite this dynamic, Lenin viewed the upcoming congress from the standpoint of a "professional revolutionary" determined to place political principle and organizational coherence above purely personal factors; he wanted this to be the case not only within the RSDLP as a whole, but also within the influential current of which he was a part, associated with the newspaper *Iskra*. Particularly among the leadership of the *Iskra* current—including Plekhanov, Axelrod, Zasulich, Martov, Potresov, and himself, who made up the paper's editorial board—relations had a "family character" marked by "painful, long-drawn-out, hopeless quarrels ... which were often repeated, making it impossible for us [to] work for *months* on end." The idea that personal quarrels would dominate over political considerations and that policies affecting the entire organization would be settled by "arrangements among ourselves" within "the old family editorial board" was intolerable to him. He wanted to ensure that "in the Party, on its formal basis, with subordination of *everything* to the Rules," such a situation would be "absolutely impossible, both judicially and morally."[25]

To advance this development, Lenin made it clear that he would call for the election at the 1903 party congress of *Iskra*'s editorial board, and also that he would propose the reduction of the board from six to three— Plekhanov, Martov, and himself. These three had done the bulk of the writing and editorial work, and each represented a distinctive element within the RSDLP leadership; that there would be three instead of six also ensured that decision-making deadlocks could be overcome by a majority vote. As he explained later to Potresov: "I consider this trio the *only* businesslike arrangement, the *only* one capable of being an official institution, instead of a body based on indulgence and slackness, the *only* one to be a real center, each member of which, I repeat, would always state and defend his party view, *not one grain more*, and irrespective of all personal motives, *all* considerations concerning grievances, resignations, and so on."[26] We can see here that Lenin had no objection to *political* disagreements arising in the party and among its leaders, that in fact he expected that all comrades would "always state and defend" their particular party viewpoint. But he wanted to see commonly accepted organizational rules, which would ensure "business-like" functioning, filtering out "personal motives" as a major factor in party life.

Another aspect of this outlook can be seen in Lenin's attitude toward the party congress, vividly described by Krupskaya: "He always, as long as he lived, attached tremendous importance to party congresses. He held the party congress to the highest authority, where all things personal had to be cast aside, where nothing was to be concealed, and everything was to be open and above board. He always took great pains in preparing

for speeches."[27] While everyone at the Second Congress of the RSDLP
subscribed in general to these organizational principles, however, many
were shocked by the thoroughgoing application that Lenin proposed.
Historian Neil Harding has noted:

> What Lenin failed to take into account was the immense emotional
> and psychological hurt that this entailed for Axelrod and Zasulich in
> particular. Earlier in the debate over Article I (defining membership),
> Plekhanov had openly ridiculed Axelrod's objections to Lenin's
> formulations, pouring public scorn on the man who had, for so long,
> been his friend and who had been so utterly dependent upon him.
> Now the final blow was to deprive him of that one mark of prestige
> which might have given him sorely needed esteem in the eyes of
> the movement and recognition of a lifetime devoted to it. Much the
> same would have applied to Zasulich and Potresov... Martov rallied
> to their defense, as they had earlier supported him, and categorically
> refused to serve on the editorial board which was, nonetheless,
> ratified by the majority.[28]

Krupskaya later recalled:

> Many were inclined to blame Plekhanov's tactlessness, Lenin's
> "vehemence" and "ambition," Pavlovich's pinpricks, and the unfair
> treatment of Zasulich and Axelrod—and they sided with those
> who had a grievance. They missed the substance through looking
> at personalities... And the substance was this—that the comrades
> grouped around Lenin were far more seriously committed to
> principles, which they wanted to see applied at all cost and pervading
> all the practical work. The other group had more of the man-in-
> the-street mentality, were given to compromise and concessions in
> principle, and had more regard for persons.[29]

After the congress, Lenin wrote to a concerned comrade:

> The story goes that the "praetorians" ousted people because of a
> slanderous accusation of opportunism, that they cast slurs on and
> removed people, etc. That is mere idle talk, the fruit of an imaginary
> grievance, *rien de plus* (nothing more). No one, absolutely no one had
> "slurs" cast upon him or was removed, prevented from taking part
> in the work. Some one or other was merely removed from the *central*

body—is that a matter for offense? Should the Party be torn apart for
that? Should a theory of (Lenin's) hypercentralism be constructed
on that account? Should there be talk of rule by rod of iron, etc., on
that account?[30]

Despite Lenin's pained objections, this is exactly what was said and
repeated far and wide by his Menshevik adversaries, who organized a
fierce campaign to disrupt RSDLP activities until the decisions of the
congress were overturned. Plekhanov abandoned the Bolsheviks, and
Lenin himself was forced off the editorial board of *Iskra*.[31] Lenin went
on to organize a Bolshevik faction around the organizational perspectives
to which he had won the 1903 congress, and he wrote *One Step Forward,
Two Steps Back* in order to explain what had happened and to clarify the
disputed organizational questions.

It was at this point that Rosa Luxemburg took the field against Lenin,
in an essay more influenced by the accounts of prestigious Mensheviks
than by the actual policies of Lenin.

LUXEMBURG'S CRITIQUE AND LENIN'S REPLY

Much of Luxemburg's polemic against Lenin consists of interpretations
that simply cannot hold up under the weight of the facts. This becomes
clear if we go through it point by point while referring to Lenin's generally
ignored point-by-point reply to her.

Luxemburg writes that *One Step Forward, Two Steps Back* "is a
methodical exposition of the ideas of the ultracentralist tendency in the
Russian movement. The viewpoint is that of pitiless centralism." Lenin
complains that Luxemburg's article

> does not acquaint the reader with my book, but with something
> else . . . Comrade Luxemburg says, for example, that my book is a
> clear and detailed expression of the point of view of "intransigent
> centralism." Comrade Luxemburg thus supposes that I defend one
> system of organization against another. But actually that is not so.
> From the first to the last page of my book, I defend the elementary
> principles of any conceivable system of party organization. My
> book is not concerned with the difference between one system
> of organization and another, but with how any system is to be

maintained, criticized, and rectified in a manner consistent with the party idea.[32]

Luxemburg writes: "Lenin's thesis is that the party Central Committee should have the privilege of naming all the local committees of the party... It should have the right to impose on all of them its own ready-made rules of conduct."[33] Lenin replies:

> Actually that is not so. What my views on this subject are can be documentarily proved by the draft Rules of Party Organization which I proposed. In that draft there is nothing about any right to organize the local committees. That right was introduced into the Party Rules by the commission elected by the (1903) Party Congress to frame them, and the Congress adopted the commission's text...In this commission which gave the Central Committee the right to organize the local committees, it was my opponents who had the upper hand.[34]

Luxemburg writes:

> The two principles on which Lenin's centralism rests are precisely these: (1) The blind subordination, in the smallest detail, of all party organs, to the party center, which alone thinks, guides, and decides for all. (2) The rigorous separation of the organized nucleus of revolutionaries from its social revolutionary surroundings. Such centralism is the mechanical transposition of the organizational principles of Blanquism into the mass movement of the socialist working class.[35]

Blanquism, named after the nineteenth-century revolutionary Auguste Blanqui, was a non-Marxist conception of revolution, to be made by conspiracies of a small revolutionary elite instead of by the self-conscious working class. Lenin responds:

> She has confused the defense of a specific point relating to a specific clause of the Rules (in that defense I was by no means intransigent, for I did not object at the plenary session to the amendment made by the commission) with the defense of the thesis (truly "ultra-centralist," is it not?) that Rules adopted by a Party congress must be adhered to until amended by a subsequent congress. This thesis (a "purely

Blanquist" one, as the reader may readily observe) I did indeed defend in my book quite "intransigently." Comrade Luxemburg says that in my view "the Central Committee is the only active nucleus of the Party." Actually that is not so. I have never advocated any such view.[36]

He went on to offer a succinct summary of what he believed the 1903 split had been about:

> Our controversy has principally been over whether the Central Committee and Central Organ should represent the trend of the majority of the Party Congress, or whether they should not. About this "ultra-centralist" and "purely Blanquist" demand the worthy comrade says not a word, she prefers to declaim against mechanical subordination of the part to the whole, against slavish submission, blind obedience, and other such bogeys. I am very grateful to Comrade Luxemburg for explaining the profound idea that slavish submission is very harmful to the Party, but I should like to know: does the comrade consider it normal for supposed party central institutions to be dominated by the minority of the Party Congress?[37]

According to Luxemburg, Lenin "is convinced that all the conditions necessary for the formation of a powerful and centralized party already exist in Russia."[38] Lenin replies:

> The thesis I advanced and advance expresses something else: I insisted, namely, that all the conditions already exist for expecting Party Congress decisions to be observed, and that the time was passed when a Party institution could be supplanted by a private circle.[39]

Lenin also responded ably to Luxemburg's charges that he wanted to impose "the regulated docility" of factory discipline inside the party and that he was a self-proclaimed Jacobin who confused this with Marxism.[40] The factory and Jacobin analogies, he pointed out, were introduced into the debate by Mensheviks, and his direct responses to them were being distorted by Luxemburg.[41]

LUXEMBURG AS "VANGUARDIST"

Having cleared away various false arguments, we are almost ready to confront the substantive challenge to Lenin's outlook that Luxemburg raises. First, however, we should take note of the common ground shared by the two revolutionaries, which is far more considerable than is generally acknowledged. In fact, much of what Luxemburg has written seems like an elaboration of the Leninist conception of the party. Even in her 1904 polemic, she stresses the need for "a proletarian vanguard, conscious of its class interests and capable of self-direction in political activity." This "self-direction" she also calls "social-democratic centralism," which she defines as the "'self-centralism' of the advanced sectors of the proletariat. It is the rule of the majority within its own party." Far from denigrating organization on behalf of "spontaneity," she insists on the need for a party which "possesses the gift of political mobility, complemented by unflinching loyalty to principles and concern for unity."[42]

Two years later, in her classic *The Mass Strike: The Political Party and the Trade Unions*—often interpreted (mistakenly) as a "spontaneist" document—she wrote:

> The social democrats are the most enlightened, most class-conscious vanguard of the proletariat. They cannot and dare not wait, in a fatalist fashion, with folded arms for the advent of the "revolutionary situation," to wait for that which in every spontaneous people's movement, falls from the clouds. On the contrary, they must now, as always, hasten the development of things and endeavor to accelerate events . . . If the widest proletarian layer should be won for a political mass action of the social democrats, and if, vice versa, the social democrats should seize and maintain the real leadership of a mass movement—should they become, in a *political sense*, the rulers of the whole movement, then we must, with the utmost clearness, consistency and resoluteness, inform the German proletariat of their tactics and aims in the general period of the coming struggle.[43]

After the Russian Revolution of 1917, in her sympathetic critique of Bolshevik policy, Luxemburg was to repeat these eminently "vanguardist" assertions in 1918, though perhaps even more forcefully: "Thus it is clear that in every revolution, only that party is capable of seizing the leadership and power which has the courage to issue the appropriate watchwords for driving the revolution ahead, and the courage to draw all the necessary conclusions from the situation."[44] Particularly scornful of the Mensheviks, Luxemburg noted that only the Bolsheviks were able to grasp "the true dialectic of revolutions" and to stand the "wisdom of parliamentary moles on its head: not through a majority to revolutionary tactics, but through revolutionary tactics to a majority—that is the way the road runs. Only a party which knows how to lead, that is, to advance things, wins support in stormy times . . . Whatever a party could offer of courage, revolutionary farsightedness and consistency in a historic hour, Lenin, Trotsky and the other comrades have given in good measure."[45]

LUXEMBURG'S CHALLENGE

We are now in a position to examine the substantive disagreement between Lenin and Luxemburg. Despite the underlying similarity in outlooks, there is an element in Luxemburg's 1904 critique of Lenin that is inconsistent with one of his fundamental premises.

The leading Menshevik Julius Martov, calling for a "broad Social Democratic working-class party," had argued: "The more widespread the title of Party member the better. We could only rejoice if every striker, every demonstrator, answering for his actions, could proclaim himself a Party member."[46] Lenin disagreed with this conception because "the borderline of the Party remains absolutely vague. . . Its harm is that it introduces a *disorganizing* idea, the confusing of class and party."[47]   In *One Step Forward, Two Steps Back,* he elaborated: "The stronger our Party organizations, consisting of *real* Social Democrats, the less wavering there is *within* the Party, the more varied, richer, and more fruitful will be the Party's influence on the elements of the *masses* surrounding it and guided by it. The Party, at the vanguard of the working class, must not be confused, after all, with the entire class."[48]

At one point in her polemic, Luxemburg says precisely the opposite: "The fact is that the social democracy is not *joined* to the organization of the proletariat. It is itself the proletariat."[49] This appears to be inconsistent, as well, with the thrust of her own "vanguardist" inclination, which has been documented. But it is an assertion related to another key point to which she gives particular stress: "The social-democratic movement cannot allow the erection of an air-tight partition between the class-conscious nucleus of the proletariat already in the party and its immediate popular environment, the nonparty sections of the proletariat." The attempt to safeguard revolutionary principles by stressing the distinction between the vanguard and the class as a whole, and efforts to establish an organizational structure reinforcing that distinction, can make the party not a living expression of the working class, but a sterile sect. "Stop that natural pulsation of a living organism, and you weaken it, and you diminish its resistance and combative spirit—in this instance, not only against opportunism but also (and that is certainly of great importance) against the existing social order. The proposed means turn against the end they are supposed to serve."[50]

The essence of Luxemburg's 1904 critique, as we can see, is the opposite of the point put forward by many latter-day anti-Leninists who appeal to her authority. She is not saying that the kind of party Lenin is building will establish a bureaucratic dictatorship once it makes a revolution. Rather, she is saying that it is in danger of degenerating into a sect, which will be *incapable of making a revolution*! Lenin sees the party not as *embracing* the working class, but as *interacting* with it for the purpose of influencing it to go in a revolutionary direction. For Luxemburg, in the passage cited above, the point is to blend into the working class as it exists, the better to contribute to its organic development as a revolutionary force.

A problem with the organizational perspective which Luxemburg appears to be proposing here is that she offers no clear alternatives to Lenin's orientation except for the organizational form of the German SPD, with its growing bureaucratic conservatism and opportunism (which she was more keenly aware of than Lenin). But she concluded that such a development arises "out of unavoidable social conditions" and "appears to be a product and an inevitable phase of the historic development of the labor movement." The problem would be corrected, she seemed to feel, by the crises of capitalist society and by the working-class radicalism and upsurges generated by those crises. "Marxist theory offers us a reliable instrument enabling us to recognize and combat typical manifestations of opportunism," she wrote. At the same time, "the working class demands the right to make its mistakes and learn in the dialectic of history."[51]

THE TEST OF HISTORY

The sectarian potential in Lenin's conception which Luxemburg identified soon became evident in 1905. The network of Bolshevik committees, "professional revolutionaries" distinct from the Russian working class, proved to be ill-prepared for the tumultuous, unplanned revolutionary upsurge which pushed tsarism to the brink of the abyss. The stalwart Bolshevik "committeemen" were blind to the revolutionary potential of the mass workers' movement led by Father Gapon, were resistant to the workers' struggles for immediate demands and to the upsurge of trade unionism, were skeptical about the value of democratic nonparty committees (soviets) of the workers, and were resistant to allowing too many radicalizing but "untempered" workers into the Bolshevik organizations. The pressure of events—combined with Lenin's own unrelenting attacks on his comrades' sectarian inclinations—gradually forced the Bolsheviks to shift on all of these questions and, by the end of 1905, to become an effective revolutionary force. But it became clear that Luxemburg's warning was not entirely unwarranted.[52]

When the Bolsheviks embraced democratic centralism in 1906, special emphasis was put on the democratic component which, as Lenin saw it, would result in "a less rigid, more 'free,' more 'loose' organization," involving "a decisive step towards the full application of the democratic principle in Party organization." Favoring the dramatic influx of working-class militants (Bolshevik membership swelled from perhaps 4,000 in 1905 to about 46,000 in 1907), Lenin explained: "We are profoundly convinced that the workers' Social Democratic organizations must be united, but in these united organizations there must be wide and free discussion of Party questions, free comradely criticism and assessments of events in Party life." In short, there must be "the principles of democratic centralism, guarantees for the rights of all minorities and for all loyal opposition, the autonomy of every Party organization, . . . recognizing that all Party functionaries must be elected, accountable to the Party and subject to recall."[53]

None of this contradicted the points that Lenin made in 1903–4 regarding the subordination of personal considerations to party rules and to majority decisions of the party congress; if anything, the policy of strengthening party democracy contributed to the realization of these points, while also contributing to the overcoming of the sectarian tendencies which had cropped up.

Even with this, however, the sectarian impulse surfaced again in 1907–11, under the leadership of such prominent Bolsheviks as Alexander Bogdanov, Leonid Krassin, Anatoly Lunacharsky, and others concerned to defend Bolshevik "purity" against a Lenin who was inclined to "entangle" the party in trade union, reform, and electoral activities. Krupskaya later recalled: "A Bolshevik, they declared, should be hard and unyielding. Lenin considered this view fallacious. It would mean giving up all practical work, standing aside from the masses instead of organizing them on real-life issues."[54] As Gregory Zinoviev put it:

> Comrade Lenin's main idea was that we had to remain with the working class and be a mass party and not to coop ourselves up exclusively in the underground and turn into a narrow circle. If the workers are in the trade unions then we must be there too; if we can send just one man into the Tsar's Duma then we shall: let him tell the workers the truth and we can publish his speeches as leaflets. If something can be done for the workers in the workers' clubs then we shall be there. We have to use every legal opportunity, so as not to divorce ourselves from the masses . . .[55]

Rejecting such "semi-Menshevik" perspectives, the ultralefts led by Bogdanov maintained their commitment to a "true Bolshevism" which was in many ways similar to what Luxemburg had criticized. An organizational split with Lenin was followed by their evolution into a sect, which soon disintegrated.

The Leninist Bolsheviks, on the other hand, became the most cohesive revolutionary force in the Russian working class from 1912 to 1914. Despite fierce repression with the onset of World War I, they made an impressive comeback with the overthrow of tsarism. By the middle of 1917 they were able to begin winning a working-class majority to the goal of socialist revolution, which was accomplished in October/November.[56]

The trajectory of Rosa Luxemburg's own SDKPiL was less fortunate. The high degree of centralization helped it to remain intact and become an effective force during the 1905 upsurge. From 1904 to 1906 its membership grew from 1,500 to 40,000. Yet it made no programmatic or organizational shifts. Robert Blobaum recounts how the SDKPiL failed to evolve in the manner that was to bring success to the Bolsheviks:

> Always the realist, Lenin was to argue that a revolutionary party had to take into consideration the existing social conditions in the empire if it wished to broaden its political base. It should therefore appeal to the nonurban masses who made up a substantial majority of the population; it should reject the sectarian approach to nonparty workers, leaving a door open to them primarily through trade union activity; and it should identify itself, however vaguely, with the national aspirations of the non-Russian sections of the population. On all of these issues, the SDKPiL was much less flexible, opting for the continuation of strict conspiratorial tactics, rigid organizational discipline, and "proletarian internationalist" positions that had characterized its recent past.[57]

Over the next several years it succumbed to sectarian isolation and debilitating splits. As it turned out, Luxemburg's polemical diagnosis of 1904 was even more apt in regard to her own organization than it was in regard to Lenin's.

No less instructive was Luxemburg's fate inside the German SPD, where she followed an orientation more consistent with her 1904 polemic. Luxemburg and her revolutionary comrades found themselves trapped in the left wing of a bureaucratized mass party which, when World War I erupted in 1914, supported the imperialist war effort instead of organizing working-class resistance. In the aftermath of the war, as the working-class radicalization foreseen by Luxemburg gathered momentum, the SPD bureaucracy was able to divert much of the proletarian militancy into "safe" channels; Luxemburg and the most determined revolutionaries were first blocked and finally ejected, left without an adequate revolutionary instrument of their own. In the midst of a rising proletarian ferment and counterrevolutionary violence, they were forced to begin rebuilding an organization.[58]

That this experience, combined with the 1917 achievement of the Bolsheviks, had an impact on her thinking should be clear from the 1918 comments of hers already quoted. There is also the testimony of those who knew her. For example, Karl Kautsky—her erstwhile comrade turned bitter opponent—noted in 1921 (two years after her death) that "in the course of the war Rosa drew steadily closer to the communist world of thought, so that it is quite correct when Radek says that 'with Rosa Luxemburg there died the greatest and most profound theoretical head of communism.'"[59] Indeed, as early as 1916 one of her closest coworkers, Karl Liebknecht, complained that her organizational orientation had become "too mechanically centralist," with "too much 'discipline,' too little spontaneity"—which sounded, as Michael Löwy has commented, like "a distant and paradoxical echo of the criticisms that Rosa herself had made in another context, addressed to Lenin."[60]

CONCLUSIONS

The purpose of this essay is by no means to shrug off the insights in Luxemburg's essay "Organizational Questions of Russian Social Democracy." The bureaucratic-sectarian tendency to which she directs our attention, while not an iron law, was very real among Lenin's Bolsheviks, and Lenin himself was forced to confront and combat it time after time. It also cropped up in Luxemburg's own Polish Marxist organization, and it has been an ever stronger tendency among many self-styled "Leninist" organizations and grouplets that have proliferated like mushrooms over the past seven decades.[61] The truth that Luxemburg insists on has, therefore, a great resonance even in our own time.

What is being suggested, however, is that it makes little historical sense to counterpose "Luxemburgism" to "Leninism" in regard to the question of revolutionary organization. More fruitful both for Marxist historians and activists would be a critical-minded integration of "Luxemburgist" into Leninist insight and experience.

5

THE CHALLENGE OF
REVOLUTIONARY DEMOCRACY

Rosa Luxemburg's remarkable life and vibrant intelligence have illuminated the human experience and inspired so many people who have reached for a better world that she must be placed within the very heart of the Marxist tradition. At the same time, many of her insights and inclinations seem to place her in advance, on certain essential matters, of even co-thinkers or partial co-thinkers (whether Kautsky, or Lenin, or Trotsky) who are also central to the Marxist tradition. This comes through, I think, in the way she talks about the natural world, in her sense of kinship with other creatures of this planet, in her open and penetrating engagement with human dignity and human suffering, in her often luminously sensual formulations and turns of phrase, and also in her wonderful humor. Her writings are incredibly alive. The fact remains that Marxism was central to what she was, just as what she was would become central to Marxism.[1]

Bertolt Brecht once wrote a poem about Luxemburg after she had been assassinated by right-wing death squads in 1919:

Red Rosa now has vanished too.
Where she lies is hid from view.
She told the poor what life's about.
And so now the rich have rubbed her out.[2]

And yet, again and again since her death, the spirit and ideas of Red Rosa have returned. In our own time, however, especially with the twentieth century's final decade, there have been renewed and incredibly powerful efforts to rub out Rosa Luxemburg altogether, as part of a well-orchestrated effort to see that Marxism itself be made to vanish as a force for understanding and changing the world.

There are some of us who do not accept that. But the only way to make this wonderful comrade live again is to refuse to be content with simply "honoring her memory" or with detailing her ideas as if we were placing the corpses of varieties of butterflies in a glass case. Rather, we must embrace, as critically and honestly as we can, the challenge of her ideas for our own time. This challenge (and especially the challenge of revolutionary democracy) is poignantly relevant to all countries, from Russia to Poland, from Germany to the United States, from Japan to China to India, from South Africa to Cuba to Brazil. Rosa Luxemburg and revolutionary Marxism live to the extent that they are absorbed into our own thoughts and actions as we struggle against oppressive realities of our own time.

Luxemburg stands as a powerful challenge to a number of false conceptions very prevalent today regarding both Marxism and democracy. Among the most powerful and influential ideologists in the world today are those who tell us that the market economy and democracy (that is, capitalism and rule by the people) historically and naturally develop hand in hand and that it is not possible, for any length of time, to have one without the other. If Rosa Luxemburg were here today, she would argue incisively and persuasively (as she did in her own time) that this is a lie. It is just as much of a falsehood as the myth that has been propagated by pro-capitalist propagandists as well as all too many would-be communists that socialism is something to be brought about through authoritarian measures.

We should deal with these two myths one at a time.

The natural development of the market economy, of capitalism (regardless of whether one views it as in some ways positive or "progressive"), is certainly authoritarian. It is based upon, and it further enhances, inequality of economic power, which naturally generates an inequality of political power. There is nothing so authoritarian as a capitalist workplace, whose function is to manage the exploitation of large numbers of workers, and this is so regardless of whether that authoritarianism assumes either brutal or benign postures. And the capitalist marketplace functions, primarily, not to meet the needs of the great majority of the people (the consumers) but rather to maximize the profits of the small minority that owns and controls the economy.[3]

If she were here, Luxemburg would also focus our attention on the actual dynamics of capitalist development in Central and Eastern Europe—the Germany, Poland, and Russia with which she was so familiar. There, for the most part, the capitalist class, sensing a greater kinship with the elites above them than with the masses below them, deferred to and intertwined with the traditional elites that were inclined to maintain authoritarianism as the political framework within which the market economy and industrial modernization would be allowed to flourish.[4]

Red Rosa would point out to us (as she did in her own day) that democracy can be advanced only through the struggles of the growing working-class majority, only through the self-organization of working people through mass movements for social and political reform, through strong, independent, democratic trade unions, through democratic mass working-class parties. Historically, it was not the normal functioning of the capitalist market, but rather the mass pressure and mass struggle of the working class movement and its allies that paved the way, step-by-step, for the expansion of democratic rights, democratic reforms, and democratic political structures.[5]

At the same time, Luxemburg was insistent that capitalism and democracy are incompatible, that in many ways the natural functioning of the capitalist market-place and of the capitalist class result in proliferating restrictions, manipulations, corruptions, erosions that undermine the gains of the working class and prevent (and must always prevent) the blossoming of a fully democratic society. And she was critical (and would be critical now) of currents in the labor and socialist movements that deny or forget that capitalism and democracy are incompatible.

Luxemburg also observed—and brilliantly analyzed—the powerful expansionist tendencies of capitalism. These resulted in the invasion of more and more portions of the globe, violating the cultures, the quality of life, and the self-determination of innumerable peoples for the benefit of capitalist enterprises that were compelled to reach for ever-expanding markets, raw materials, and investment opportunities. This authoritarian process of global capital accumulation, defined as imperialism, was also dependent on the expansion of exceptionally authoritarian military machines. The aggressive expansionism and growing militarism would, as Luxemburg so correctly predicted, result in violent catastrophes (colonial wars, world wars, and more) in which the masses of people would pay the price, for the benefit of wealthy and powerful elites. She warned that such developments might also whirl out of control and threaten the future of civilization itself.[6]

Against this triumph of authoritarianism, violence, and death, Luxemburg passionately struggled for the socialist alternative. In her view, the socialist movement had proved to be the most consistent force for democracy in the world, and this view has received considerable support from knowledgeable and serious historians in recent years. More than this, she viewed socialism quite simply as an expanded, deepened, authentic democracy—genuine rule by the people in both the political and economic life of society. Her notion of a workers' state (what has sometimes been called "dictatorship of the proletariat") had nothing to do with a one-party dictatorship ruling in the name of the people. Rather, it meant what Marx and Engels said in the *Communist Manifesto* when they spoke of the working class winning the battle of democracy, what Lenin meant in *The State and Revolution*, when he spoke of a thoroughgoing political rule by the working class. This was in contrast to the authoritarian political forms that began to develop all too soon in the wake of the 1917 Russian Revolution.[7]

Luxemburg was an early critic of this development, challenging Lenin and the Bolsheviks (whom she held in high esteem) to pull back from their dangerously expansive justifications for the undemocratic emergency measures that were adopted in the face of both internal counterrevolutionary assaults and a global capitalist counteroffensive. "Freedom only for the supporters of the government, only for the members of one party—however numerous they may be—is no freedom at all," she insisted. "Freedom is always and exclusively freedom for the one who thinks differently."[8] In her prophetic warning, she elaborated:

> Without general elections, without unrestricted freedom of press and assembly, without a free struggle of opinion, life dies out in every public institution, becomes a mere semblance of life, in which only the bureaucracy remains as the active element. Public life gradually falls asleep, a few dozen party leaders of inexhaustible energy and boundless experience direct and rule. Among them, in reality only a dozen outstanding heads do the leading and an elite of the working class is invited from time to time to meetings where they are to applaud the speeches of the leaders, and to approve proposed

resolutions unanimously—at bottom, then, a clique affair—a dictatorship, to be sure, not the dictatorship of the proletariat, however, but only the dictatorship of a handful of politicians.[9]

Luxemburg was also profoundly critical of authoritarian developments of a different sort inside her own Social Democratic Party of Germany. An increasingly powerful group inside the party and trade union leadership was arguing that the gradual accumulation of reforms—to painlessly erase capitalism's worst features—would be a better path for achieving socialist goals. Luxemburg responded that it was not possible to choose different paths to socialism in the same way that one might choose either spicy sausages or mild sausages in the market. The reformist path, she prophetically insisted, would not lead gradually to socialism at all, but to the gradual accommodation and subjugation of the socialist movement to the authoritarian proclivities, the brutal realities, and the violent dynamics of the capitalist system. Even though vital gains could be won for the working class through struggles for reforms, this would be like the labor of Sisyphus—the strong man in the ancient Greek myth who time after time would roll a heavy boulder up a steep hill, only to have the gods roll it back down again. So would the natural dynamics of capitalism time after time outflank and erode the reforms won by the labor movement.[10]

Luxemburg taught that in order to remain true to its democratic and socialist principles, and in order to defend the material interests of the workers and the oppressed, the socialist workers' movement—even while fighting for necessary and life-giving partial reforms—would sometimes find itself in uncompromising confrontation with the capitalist power structure. What she and her revolutionary-minded comrades found, however, is that the increasingly bureaucratized structure of their own socialist workers' movement was becoming an obstacle to the internal democracy of the movement. The increasingly bureaucratic-conservative leadership of the trade unions and party more and more sought to contain radicalizing impulses of the working-class membership, to limit the ability of people such as Luxemburg to present a revolutionary socialist perspective, to deflect upsurges in the class struggle into safely moderate channels. They sought to maintain the reformist strategy that they sincerely believed was more "practical," but which was, in fact, entwining the labor movement into the authoritarian structures and disastrous directions of the capitalist status quo.[11]

Rosa Luxemburg was quite clear that the majority of the people—and the working class as such—were by no means uniformly or consistently inclined to go in a revolutionary or socialist direction. She saw political and social consciousness among the masses of people as incredibly deep and diverse, contradictory, and shifting, tending to go in one direction at one point and then in a very different direction soon after. The oppressive and sometimes horrific nature of capitalist development, however, when combined with the clear and capable articulation of perspectives of class struggle and socialism, could sometimes cause dramatic upsurges—what she called mass strikes, or mass actions, that would often take place outside of existing structures of the labor movement. She saw this, in part, as essential in the creation of militant new trade unions and other organizations of the workers and oppressed, although its implications went further. Luxemburg had no desire to deny the importance of the day-to-day work of the existing trade unions and of the votes cast by the socialist representatives elected to Germany's parliament. But a movement capable of actually attaining socialism must go beyond this. It was essential, she believed, that a proliferation of possibilities be found to engage more and more people in action, in experiences that would deepen their own understanding and commitment and skills, that would enhance their own confidence and creativity, as well as their ability to inspire and win ever more workers to the revolutionary cause.[12]

And this understanding was central for her as a revolutionary strategist, distinguishing her from the dominant leadership of the German Social Democratic Party. Luxemburg gave great weight to so-called "extra-parliamentary" social struggles and to a dynamic interplay between existing organizations and spontaneous mass action. This frightened her less revolutionary comrades. She put it this way:

> As bred-in-the-bone disciples of parliamentary cretinism, these German social democrats have sought to apply to revolutions the homemade wisdom of the parliamentary nursery: in order to carry anything, you must first have a majority. The same, they say, applies to the revolution: first let's become a "majority." The true dialectic of revolutions, however, stands this wisdom on its head: not through a majority to revolutionary tactics, but through revolutionary tactics to

a majority—that is the way the road runs. Only a party which knows how to lead, that is, to advance things, wins support in stormy times.[13]

For Luxemburg there was a remarkable consistency between this revolutionary-democratic strategic perspective and her revolutionary-democratic vision of socialism. Here is how she put it:

Bourgeois class rule has no need of the political training and education of the entire mass of the people, at least not beyond certain narrow limits. But for the proletarian dictatorship that is the life element, the very air without which it is not able to exist. . . . Only experience is capable of correcting and opening new ways. Only unobstructed, effervescing life falls into a thousand new forms and improvisations, brings to light creative force, itself corrects all mistaken attempts. . . . The whole mass of the people must take part. . . . Socialism in life demands a complete spiritual transformation in the masses degraded by centuries of class rule. Social instincts in place of egotistical ones, mass initiative in place of inertia, idealism which conquers all suffering. . . . The only way to a rebirth is the school of public life itself, the most unlimited, the broadest democracy and public opinion.[14]

It is obvious that such genuine democracy as Rosa Luxemburg believed in cannot be bestowed on a people through charismatic leaders, through well-meaning revolutionary elites, through single-party dictatorships, through labor bureaucracies, through glitzy election campaigns financed by big-business interests, and certainly not through military invasions from powerful outsiders. It must be won through the accumulation of experience and struggles, also the proliferation of seasoned activists and democratic organizations, and the consequent rise of consciousness and revolutionary-democratic commitment among the masses of the people themselves, especially the immense majority of those who labor.[15]

And people such as ourselves—all who labor, as well as all who identify with those who labor—must face the difficult question of whether we want to help advance such a process, and if so, how.

6

HEART OF DARKNESS

"Imperialism," Rosa Luxemburg tells us, "is the political expression of the process of the accumulation of capital in its competitive struggle over the unspoiled remainder of the noncapitalist world environment."[1]

With the publication in English of *The Complete Works of Rosa Luxemburg*, starting with two volumes of her major economic writings, it will become possible—perhaps imperative—to integrate ever more of her insights into our efforts to comprehend the violent dynamics of our own time by tracing them back to the swirling realities of hers. The purpose of her 1913 magnum opus, *The Accumulation of Capital: A Contribution to the Economic Theory of Imperialism*, was (as explained in its recently translated foreword) to advance "our practical struggle against imperialism."[2] Her uncompromising analysis even dared to take issue with formulations offered by Marx himself. It so unsettled many of her more moderate socialist comrades that they unleashed an unrelenting barrage of criticism against it.

A fundamental violation of their perceptions had been committed. They believed in an inevitable upward swirl of Progress culminating in the liberation of humanity. Their way of understanding Marxism posited a positive mission of Europe's industrial capitalism, reaching all around the world, drawing humanity together and lifting up the peoples of all countries—in spite of everything—to the grandeur of a socialist future.

In works of art, however, including some of humanity's most compelling literature, we can find imagery and insights—reflecting the lived experience of honest writers—that go deeper than what harmony-minded optimists are capable of, intersecting instead with the dark and urgent perceptions of Rosa Luxemburg.

THE HORROR

Shortly before the appearance of her own masterpiece, Joseph Conrad composed one of the classic short novels in the English language, *Heart of Darkness*, which focused precisely on the horrific realities with which Luxemburg dealt so eloquently. Even such severe critics as Chinua Achebe and Edward Said have described this novella as the work of "one of the great stylists of modern fiction," in which "the imperial attitude is . . . beautifully captured in . . . complicated and rich narrative form."[3] Exploring aspects of this fictional work may throw Luxemburg's own insights into sharp relief.

As Achebe tells us, the sensibilities of Conrad's characters—indeed, of the narrative in which they are embedded, and of Conrad himself—are permeated with the racism characteristic of the imperialist metropolis of old turn-of-the-century Europe. Central to such sensibilities is the violation of Achebe's own homeland—"the dehumanization of Africa and Africans." For Achebe, *Heart of Darkness* is a morality tale of what happens "when things leave their accustomed place, like Europe leaving its safe stronghold between the policeman and the baker to take a peep into the heart of darkness" in the vast jungles of the Congo basin. The charismatic and eloquent idealist Kurtz—boldly determined to advance the forces of progress through the extension of audacious European enterprise in the African heartland—"foolishly exposed himself to the wild irresistible allure of the jungle," becoming transformed into a sadistic mass murderer "who willfully had given his soul to the powers of darkness and 'taken a high seat amongst the devils of the land.'"[4]

The story's narrator, Marlow, journeys up the Congo River to retrieve an important official, Kurtz, employed by a substantial European company engaged in the ivory trade. A brilliant intellectual who wrote a study extolling Europe's "civilizing mission" among the savages, Kurtz has turned into a murderous tyrant—worshipped by the natives he rules over (at least those whose heads he has not impaled on many wooden stakes)—who has written the following addendum to his high-minded study: "Exterminate all the brutes." Marlow brings a seriously ill Kurtz on the steamboat back toward civilization, away from his adoring followers, including a very beautiful Black mistress, but the dying "hero" expires on the journey, after looking deep into his life, his experience, his soul, the void, and gasping: "The horror! The horror!"[5]

The story concludes with Marlow's return to England, where he sees Kurtz's wealthy young fiancée (his Intended), seemingly the epitome of pure and virtuous womanhood, who worships the memory of her bold and idealistic hero. Marlow lies to her about Kurtz's life in Africa and about his final words. And he retreats from her in a horrified panic not explicitly explained. While many do not comment on it, there are ways in which the heroine—although seemingly oblivious to the murderous savagery of her hero—becomes one with him, herself representing the "heart of darkness."

Darkness permeates all—from "the mahogany door" to "the dusk [that] was falling" to "the dark gleams" on the grand piano (compared to a sarcophagus, its ivory keys unmentioned). The fiancée enters: "She came forward all in black with a pale head, floating toward me in the dusk." Soon "the room seemed to have grown darker," and despite the "pure brow" and "ashy halo," the fiancée's "dark eyes looked out at me." The link between Kurtz and his Intended—"his death and her sorrow"—unnerves Marlow. "I asked myself what I was doing there, with a sensation of panic in my heart as though I had blundered into a place of cruel and absurd mysteries not fit for a human being to behold." Despite her innocence (and as the room further darkens), the "pure" and pale Intended merges for Marlow with Kurtz's African mistress, with Kurtz himself, and with the horror, in which she is somehow implicated.[6] Jonah Raskin nicely captures what is going on in this "world in which progress drinks nectar from the skulls of the slain": "The Congo voyage transformed him. To discover that behind your affluence lies another man's poverty, that behind your ease lies another man's exploitation, that behind your life lies another man's death, that your fate is inextricably connected with the fate of millions of Black men and women whose existence you had denied—all this is mind-blowing. It drives Marlow mad. His madness is illuminating."[7]

STRENGTH AND SPLENDOR

In this, the Anglo-Polish novelist seems only steps away from the Polish-German revolutionary, who recognizes that the murderous savagery—covered over with idealistic pretense—had its origins not with the African victims of colonialism, but with the European homeland breeding the voracious knights of imperialism. She insists that the promise of "the great so-called works of culture that were [to be] brought to the primitive countries" is fraudulent. "To capitalist economists and politicians, railroads, matches, sewerage systems, and warehouses are progress and culture," Luxemburg scoffs. Yet "such works, grafted upon primitive conditions...are too dearly paid for with the sudden economic and cultural ruin of the peoples who must drink down the bitter cup" of imperialist violence and oppression.[8]

Dark horrors are visited upon innumerable victims in Africa, Asia, Latin America, and among indigenous peoples of Australia and North America—what Luxemburg referred to as "the unspoiled remainder of the noncapitalist world environment."[9] These are generated, as she demonstrates in The Accumulation of Capital, from the very heart of European civilization, permeated and animated as it is by the capital accumulation process.

Like Marx, Luxemburg understood capitalism as an expansive system driven by the dynamic of accumulation. Capital in the form of money is invested in commodities in the form of raw materials and tools and labor-power, which is transformed—by the squeezing of actual labor out of the labor-power of the workers—into capital in the form of the commodities thereby produced, whose increased value is realized through the sale of the commodities for more money than was originally invested, which is the increased capital out of which the capitalist extracts his profits, only to be driven to invest more capital for the purpose of achieving ever-greater capital accumulation. She saw a voracious capital accumulation process, compelled by its very nature to expand over the entire face of the earth.

This corresponds to what exponents of imperialism in many capitalist economies were themselves explaining in the early twentieth century. "In every country which has received a high level of industrial and commercial development and . . . a surplus of capital is experienced," noted Count Sergei Witte, finance minister in Tsarist Russia, "the need for the export of capital becomes an absolute and ineluctable necessity." From a similar vantage-point, French statesman Léon Gambetta commented that "to remain a great nation, or to become one, you must colonize." Prominent British theorist Karl Pearson explained the nation must be "an organic whole . . . kept up to a high pitch of external efficiency by contest, chiefly by way of war with inferior races, and with equal races by the struggle for trade and for the sources of raw materials and food supply."[10]

Winston Churchill—absolutely committed since childhood to Britain's colonial empire—chimed in: "Let it be granted that nations exist and peoples labor to produce armies with which to conquer other nations, and the nation best qualified to do this is of course the most highly civilized and the most deserving of honor." And with an idealistic rhetoric and pale purity worthy of Kurtz and his Intended, Churchill noted: "The strength and splendor of our authority is derived not from physical forces, but from moral ascendancy, liberty, justice, English tolerance, and English honesty."[11]

At the same time, Churchill was—along with others animated by the imperial preference—hardly paralyzed by such humanitarian concerns. "We have engrossed to ourselves, in times when other powerful nations were paralyzed by barbarism or internal war, an altogether disproportionate share of the wealth and traffic of the world," he acknowledged: "We have got all we want in territory, and our claim to be left in the unmolested enjoyment of vast and splendid possessions, mainly acquired by violence, largely maintained by force, often seems less reasonable to others than to us."[12]

EVERYTHING IS PERMITTED

W. E. B. Du Bois later summarized the result: "There was no Nazi atrocity—concentration camps, wholesale maiming and murder, defilement of women or ghastly blasphemy of childhood—which the Christian civilization of Europe had not long been practicing against colored folk in all parts of the world in the name of and for the defense of a Superior Race born to rule the world."[13]

Strikingly similar were the judgments of political theorist Hannah Arendt, who traced European imperialism, with all of its murderous inhumanity, as an essential element in the crystallization of the "totalitarianism" that would bear down on European civilization in the first half of the twentieth century. (In the process, Arendt identifies Luxemburg's *Accumulation of Capital* as an important source for her own *Origins of Totalitarianism*.) Focusing precisely on the site of Conrad's novella, she wrote of "the decimation of the peaceful Congo population—from 20 to 40 million reduced to 8 million people; and finally, perhaps worst of all, it resulted in the triumphant introduction of such means of pacification into ordinary, respectable foreign policies."[14] Observing that "the extermination of native peoples went hand in hand with colonization," Arendt noted the extensive use of concentration camps "for 'undesirable elements,'" and concluded: "All this clearly points to totalitarian methods of domination; all these are elements they utilize, develop and crystallize on the basis of the nihilistic principle that 'everything is permitted.'"[15]

Luxemburg reveals imperialism's horrific and systematic inhumanity at the very heart of European civilization as shaped by the capitalist mode of production, with dynamics that can be traced to its earliest beginnings. The survey of impacts in her *Accumulation of Capital* includes the following examples:

- the destruction of the English peasants and artisans;
- the destruction of the native peoples of North America (the so-called Indians);
- the enslavement of African peoples;
- British incursions into China, with special reference to the Opium Wars;
- the ruination of small farmers in the midwestern and western regions of the United States;
- the onslaught of French colonialism in Algeria, Tunisia, and Vietnam; and
- the onslaught of British colonialism in India, Egypt, and South Africa (in the latter case with lengthy reference to the three-way struggle of Black African peoples, the Dutch Boers, and the British).

Each expansion "is accompanied by capital's relentless war on the social and economic interrelations of the indigenous inhabitants," Luxemburg writes, "and by the violent looting of their means of production and their labor power." Observing that "for the primitive societies . . . it is a question of their very existence," she notes that "the only possible course of action is to engage in resistance and a life-or-death struggle until they are completely exhausted, or exterminated," which meant she understood that the invariable consequence involved "permanent military occupation of the colonies, indigenous risings, and expeditions to crush these are the order of the day for any colonial regime."[16]

The economic underpinnings of such realities are always emphasized in her work: "The means of production and labor-power of these formations, as well as their demand for the capitalist surplus product, are indispensible to capitalism itself. In order to wrest these means of production and this labor-power from these formations, and to convert them into purchasers of its commodities, capitalism strives purposefully to annihilate them as independent social structures."[17] But the destructive impact of all this on the cultures of the world's peoples was emphasized by Luxemburg as by no other Marxist theorist of her time: "The ravenous greed, the voracious appetite for accumulation, the very essence of which is to take advantage of each new political and economic conjuncture with no thought for tomorrow, precludes any appreciation of the value of the works of economic infrastructure that have been left by previous civilizations."[18] We see the equivalent, on a massive and systematic scale, of ancient barbarians and modern-day fanatics tearing apart innocent communities while torching and smashing to pieces priceless cultural treasures, bringing to mind Luxemburg's admonition that we must choose between "socialism or barbarism."[19]

IMPERIALISM OR BARBARISM?

Luxemburg's contention was the exact opposite of the truth—at least from the standpoint of educated opinion dominant in much of the world. The British Empire was at the apex of imperialism in its colonial incarnation, "much larger than anything created by the Romans, the Persians, the Mughals, the Spaniards in the Americas or even by the Chinese" in days of yore. In 1922, conservative US philosopher George Santayana wrote with great enthusiasm of the British Empire: "Never since the days of heroic Greece has the world had such a sweet, just, boyish master. It will be a black day for the human race when the blackguards, churls and fanatics manage to supplant him." Latter-day historian John Bowle admonishes the long-dead Anglophile for the "wildly romanticized" breathlessness of his rhetoric, while adding, nonetheless, "many people, in principle, agree with his conclusion."[20]

In his learned and extensive reflections on *The Imperial Achievement*, Bowle is able to sum things up (after 500 pages) in a single long sentence: "Thus, spread out around the globe, the British Empire and its Commonwealth, at its greatest extent between the wars [that is, between World Wars I and II], contained a fantastic variety of countries and peoples, protected by British naval power and by bluff, wealth and the kind of credit and prestige enjoyed by a conservative, long-established business house."[21] With high-minded, Kurtz-like perceptions (referring to native cultures as "a variety of barbarisms"), Bowle explains that the empire unified much of the vast world with English, "now the most widespread world language," as well as "the rule of law," with models of parliamentary government and "efficient administration." There has been the introduction of steam power and its successors, and infrastructures involving railways, irrigation systems, modern farming techniques, medical advances, widespread education, also bringing "peoples confined to farming areas into contact with the modern world." Not to mention British sports—"the cult of football [soccer] and cricket."[22]

There is common ground between this and the manner in which a leading "moderate" socialist in Germany's Social Democratic Party, Eduard Bernstein, viewed the matter. "We will condemn and oppose certain methods of subjugating savages, but we will not condemn the idea that savages be subjugated and made to conform to the rules of a higher civilization," Bernstein wrote in 1896. He scoffed at the rash appeals of some of the more revolutionary socialists for support of armed struggle against imperialism: "To aid . . . the savages against advancing capitalist civilization, if it were feasible, which it is not, would only prolong the struggle, not prevent it." He added, two years later, "the subjection of the natives to the authority of European administration does not always entail worsening their condition, but often means the opposite." This dovetails with his conviction that the goals of socialism would be realized gradually through the socialist movement's contribution—through assisting with the accumulation of reforms—in "the general movement of society, i.e., social progress," and that "the expansion of markets and of international trade relations has been one of the most powerful levers of social progress."[23]

Bernstein emphasized that "the increase of the wealth of nations," the material basis for the socialist future, comes about precisely through the global expansion of capitalism. "The colonies are there. We must come to terms with that," Bernstein insisted during 1907 debates in the Socialist International. "Socialists too should acknowledge the need for civilized people to act somewhat like guardians of the uncivilized." He produced quotations from Karl Marx and Ferdinand Lassalle which—he claimed— supported this notion, concluding: "Our economies are based, in large measure, on the extraction from the colonies of products that the native peoples had no idea how to use."[24]

As has often been noted, Bernstein was strongly influenced by the moderate variety of non-Marxist socialists in Britain, where he had lived in exile for several years, who came to be called Fabians. These included Sidney and Beatrice Webb, George Bernard Shaw, H. G. Wells, and others. They advocated policies and practices designed to make capitalism increasingly efficient and benign, seeing this as leading, very slowly but surely, to an evolution culminating in socialism. Their approach included a high tolerance of militarism and a frank embrace of imperialism—which caused some to call them (and other liberal-minded reformers, such as the highly esteemed German sociologist Max Weber, who felt a close kinship with Bernstein) "social-imperialists."[25]

Luxemburg was hardly the only figure in the Marxist movement to challenge the kinds of things Bernstein was saying and advocating. But her revolutionary anti-imperialism went significantly further than some of her "orthodox" comrades wanted to go. Her insistence that the violence and inhumanity of the imperialist reality flowed naturally and necessarily from the capital accumulation process was much too dark for them. Even with the horrific explosion of World War I, Luxemburg's one- time friend Karl Kautsky could not accept the darkness of her vision. He had broken with her a few years earlier, to stay in the good graces of the Social Democratic Party leadership, tilting as it was toward Bernstein's orientation. He noted that for some in the Marxist movement (such as Luxemburg) "the meaning of the word imperialism has expanded so far that all the manifestations of modern capitalism are included in it," and "in that sense, naturally, imperialism is a vital necessity for capitalism."[26]

But Kautsky preferred a more limited definition: the desire of highly industrialized capitalist countries to conquer and annex agrarian zones.[27] "The extreme Right and the extreme Left of our party declare that imperialism is a necessity for the existing mode of production." Armed with his own definition, he could disagree with both. "Actually, imperialism is just a question of power, not an economic necessity," he emphasized. "Not only is it not necessary for capitalist economic life, but its significance for capitalism has in many cases been exaggerated beyond all measure." In fact, "imperialism is a particular kind of capitalist policy," and "it will pass away, it will be 'eradicated,' its decline is a necessity—the only question is when this will begin."[28]

In fact, Kautsky posited, it would be overcome by the more intelligent capitalist statesmen, who would craft a harmonious "ultra-imperialism" to replace the violence of global competition with the harmony of cooperative global capitalist development (within whose framework socialist efforts would ultimately flourish). His position would be restated influentially in the 1960s and 1970s by "democratic socialists" George Lichtheim and Michael Harrington (the latter referred to an "almost-imperialism" that could be modified by more enlightened US foreign policy choices).[29] Other variants of Kautsky's and Bernstein's orientations have been articulated in the twenty-first century as well.

LITERARY INTRANSIGENTS

An imperialist policeman named Eric Blair—who later left his post to become the angry socialist writer George Orwell—spoke with contempt of those who emphasized the benign qualities of imperialism. "In order to hate imperialism, you have to be part of it," he reflected. "Seen from the outside, British rule in India appears—indeed, it is—benevolent and even necessary; and such no doubt are the French rule in Morocco and the Dutch rule in Borneo." But seen from the inside, "it is an unjustifiable tyranny." He added: "In the police you see the dirty work of Empire at close quarters, and there is an appreciable difference between doing dirty work and merely profiting by it. . . . I had begun to have an indescribable loathing of the whole machinery of so-called justice."[30]

Such inhumanity can be found in multiple contexts, but given the very nature of imperialism, as Orwell notes, it flows inexorably from the nature of our economic system. Reflecting on the naive enthusiasm of British imperialism's great poet, Rudyard Kipling, he commented: "He could not understand what was happening, because he had never had any grasp of the economic forces underlying imperial expansion. It is notable that Kipling does not seem to realize, any more than the average soldier or colonial administrator, that an empire is primarily a money-making concern."[31] For Kipling and others of his type, imperialism is "a sort of forcible evangelizing," in which "you turn a Gatling gun on a mob of 'natives,' and then you establish 'the Law,' which includes roads, railways and a courthouse."[32] Orwell came to despise even the left-wing organizations (for example, the Labour Party, but perhaps some even further to the left) that claimed an anti-imperialist perspective:

> All left-wing parties in the highly industrialized countries are at bottom a sham, because they make it their business to fight against something which they do not wish to destroy. They have internationalist aims, and at the same time they struggle to keep up a standard of life within which those aims are incompatible. We all live by robbing Asiatic coolies, and those of us who are "enlightened" all maintain that those coolies ought to be set free; but our standard of living, and hence our "enlightenment," demands that the robbery shall continue. The humanitarian is always a hypocrite . . .[33]

It is worth noting that Orwell dared to conceive of a future society in which there could be a good life consistent with equality and freedom, and devoid of hypocrisy—a stateless society having what might be conceived of as "a low standard of living" for all. "It need not imply a hungry or uncomfortable world," he explained, "but it rules out the kind of air-conditioned, chromium-plated, gadget-ridden existence which is now considered desirable or enlightened." As George Woodcock commented, William Morris, an earlier British writer with similar libertarian socialist inclinations, projected just such a world of the free and the equal in his 1890 classic *News from Nowhere*. But the drift of Orwell's twentieth century seemed to be pulling in much darker directions.[34]

Actually the darkness inherent in modernity is vibrantly identified by two of the greatest American writers of the nineteenth century, Herman Melville and Mark Twain (Samuel Clemens)—both infected by the glowing humanistic and egalitarian promise of democracy, both disgusted by the shallow and voracious greed of capitalism, each experiencing perceptions sharpened by the imperialist horror inherent in modern human slavery. One can find such amazingly dark insights in Melville's *The Confidence Man*, of course *Moby Dick*, and certainly *Benito Cerano* (in its own way closely comparable to Conrad's *Heart of Darkness*). Twain packs them into *Huckleberry Finn, A Connecticut Yankee in King Arthur's Court*, and the savage commentaries to be found in *Mark Twain on the Damned Human Race*.[35]

A problem with crafting even the finest, if most devastating, works of art from the brutalizing exploitation and violent oppression of human beings, needless to say, is that they can (especially if achieving the status of classics) have entertainment value for the consumers of culture and enhance the reputations of the artists, thereby becoming transformed into parasitic excrescences derived from the horrors represented. The virtue of such theoretical explorations as Rosa Luxemburg's *The Accumulation of Capital* is that they are organically and directly connected to movements and struggles whose function is to eliminate the horrors altogether.

BACKDRAFT AND INSURGENCY

In the same year that saw the publication of her book, one finds, embedded in celebratory comments on the working-class holiday of May Day, Luxemburg's warning of (as she put it) "the world war which, sooner or later, is unavoidable." The systematic brutality utilized against the victims of imperialism in Asia, Africa, and Latin America, and the ever-more-powerful militarism built up to sustain the imperialist hold on masses of subject peoples in those far off continents, would soon slip out of control. Various imperialist powers increasingly pushed against each other over who would possess what in the global market. "In this moment of armament lunacy and war orgies," she insisted, "only the resolute will to struggle of the working masses, their capacity and readiness for powerful mass actions, can maintain world peace and push away the menacing world conflagration."[36]

Yet the European proletariat proved unable to prevent the dreaded world war. Voracious fires of violence, destruction, and mass murder exploded from the colonies, like a horrific backdraft, into the very heartland of once-peaceful Europe—so civilized, so highly cultured, with its pure brow and ashy halo of "progress." Among the 65 million men mobilized to fight in this so-called Great War, there were about 9 million—one soldier out of seven—combat deaths, with an additional 5 million reported missing and 7 million suffering permanent disabilities (out of approximately 21 million wounded). This was a total war, with the estimated civilian deaths resulting from the war exceeding the military casualties, with the horrendous wreckage of cities, farmlands, and countries, not to mention the brutalization of life, leaving a lasting imprint on all that followed in the twentieth century.[37]

As early as the year in which *The Accumulation of Capital* was published (1913), Vladimir Ilyich Lenin penned a brief but expansive essay entitled "The Historical Destiny of the Doctrine of Karl Marx" in which he argued that the imperialist-dominated peoples (he was focusing especially on those of Asia) were becoming central to the revolutionary strategy for advancing the goals of democracy and socialism. Pointing to proliferating anticolonial and democratic insurgencies, he insisted that "no power on earth can restore the old serfdom in Asia or wipe out the heroic democracy of the masses in the Asiatic and semi-Asiatic countries," adding: "The fact that Asia, with its population of 800 million, has been drawn into the struggle for these same European ideals, should inspire us with optimism."[38]

The explosive and horrific slaughter of World War I by no means extinguished revolutionary socialist perspectives but instead caused an increasing number of activists to fight their way to new perspectives that would build on Luxemburg's insights but go beyond them. One of these was a critical-minded Dutch Marxist, Herman Gorter, who gave special emphasis (like Lenin but oddly *not* Luxemburg) to the *self-activity* of the peoples confronting imperialist oppression:

> It makes no difference to the working class as a whole whether England or another country possesses a greater part of the world .... They should oppose capitalistic colonial policies, because they aim at a better society than this capitalistic one, a society that needs no colonies to exploit.... The colonial program of revolutionary socialism is as follows: (1) Protesting against colonial usurpation and extortion. (2) Attempting to protect and liberate the natives so long as they themselves are too weak for revolutionary action. (3) Supporting every revolutionary act of the natives and demanding their political and national independence, as soon as they begin revolutionary activity for themselves.[39]

Lenin and Gorter were revolutionary comrades of Luxemburg's, each of them engaged in the collective effort to understand and change the world.

Gorter's book, which appeared in 1914, was warmly embraced by Lenin and was dedicated to Rosa Luxemburg. While not calling for the rising of the colonial peoples, Luxemburg sought to rally the German working class to move forward as part of a global insurgency, begun in Russia in 1917, that would bring an end to imperialism altogether, by destroying the inherently destructive capitalism that was at the root of it all. A later historian, sympathetic not with the revolutionaries but with the imperial empires, expresses it all with admirable sweep:

> The First World War let loose an attempt at world revolution when a Marxist-Leninist government seized power in Russia after the collapse of the Tsarist regime. Hence a radiating attack on capital and on "bourgeois" civilization itself, which in Lenin's realistic interpretation and Trotsky's fanatical vision was interpreted in terms of a revolt, not merely of the masses in the advanced countries led by Marxist elites, but also of colonial peoples against the capitalist West and the United States.[40]

In the turmoil of 1918 and early 1919, as the German monarchy collapsed, Luxemburg and Karl Liebknecht began to win the hearts and minds of angry and insurgent workers, rallying them to the banners of the Spartacus League (named after the leader of the slave uprising against the Roman Empire), and then to the newly formed German Communist Party. But the moderate Social Democrats, still with a mass following, had made a deal with capitalists and generals and moved to establish a capitalist republic. Tagging her "bloody Rosa," they were now almost explicitly calling for her elimination and would be at least indirectly implicated in her death.[41]

Similarly, liberal-nationalist academic Max Weber, up to his elbows in political polemics, was one of many from the upper classes vociferously denouncing the revolutionaries, especially targeting their leaders with special hatred. "What is decisive now is whether the crazy Liebknecht gang will be kept down," he asserted. "Liebknecht belongs in a madhouse, and Rosa Luxemburg in a zoo." Eleven days later, paramilitary death squads went even further, amid the violent repression of the Spartacus uprising. (The paramilitary forces, the notorious Freikorps, have been seen by many as precursors to the still-gestating Nazi movement that would, within fifteen years, overwhelm the German political scene.) While publicly deploring the brutal assassinations, Weber suggested that—in trying to mobilize "the street"—the victims were themselves responsible for the murderous violence done to them.[42]

BLACK BOOKS AND HOLOCAUSTS

An interesting twist executed by a certain current within German historiography has further extended Weber's impulse, blaming the Reds for their own victimization and for the triumphant rise of Adolf Hitler. As one historian has critically summarized it: "Nazi atrocities were no worse than the earlier Bolshevik and Stalinist crimes on which they were allegedly modeled and . . . the Holocaust represented an understandable preemptive response by the Nazis to the perceived communist threat."[43]

Related to this is *The Black Book of Communism*, composed by a cluster of disillusioned ex-leftists in France, arguing that what Luxemburg and her comrades were trying to do ultimately killed 100 million people in the course of eight decades (generating tyrannical regimes opposed to human freedom and dignity). The book tells us that the communists, inhumane destroyers of life, were no better—perhaps even worse—than the Nazis. Without question, there are genuine crimes against humanity, done in the name of Communism, which these authors document. Many of those who shared Luxemburg's uncompromising critique of capitalism and commitment to a socialist/communist future of the free and the equal perished (as she did) in the battle for that future, but others presumably "won" the battle in the vast Russian Empire and elsewhere and began to build "the future"—with horrific results. George Orwell's fable *Animal Farm* satirizes some of what happened, where the dream of a better world is corrupted and betrayed by presumed "revolutionary" leaders whose new tyranny turns out no better than the old. Inhumanity and murder on a massive scale have been amply described and analyzed by some sharing (or at least sympathetic with) Luxemburg's revolutionary perceptions.[44]

But *The Black Book of Communism* is badly flawed in more ways than one. Attributing to Communism one million deaths in Vietnam, without factoring in the one million Vietnamese deaths resulting from the US war in Vietnam (it is not clear whether we are talking about the same million here) raises serious questions. There is also a more general historiographical issue related to the book's argument—approvingly highlighted by historian

Martin Malia in his foreword to the English edition of this volume—
that "there never was a benign, initial phase of communism before some
mythical 'wrong turn' threw it off track" and that the problem can really
be traced to "the 'scientific' Marxist belief in class struggle as the 'violent
midwife of history,' in Marx's famous metaphor." But independently of
Karl Marx, and long before the rise of the modern communist movement,
there actually were classes and violent class struggles, particularly as
laboring majorities were brutally subjugated and ruthlessly exploited, as
they so often were, for the purpose of enriching powerful minorities.
Such "violence of the status quo" continues to our own time, well after the
collapse of communism.[45]

Mass violence and inhumanity were the staple of the human condition
well before 1917 or 1933 and were attributable neither to communism nor
to Nazism, but to good old-fashioned imperialism—which slaughtered
many millions more, and caused intensive suffering and inhumanity
over a much greater expanse of time, than what is offered up to us in
the Black Book of Communism. Adam Hochschild reminds us that at least
10 million people perished in the killing fields of the Congo alone (the
"stomping grounds" of Joseph Conrad's Kurtz) thanks to the vicious
policies associated with King Leopold's Belgium, and Mike Davis tells us
of the imperialist-caused famines that obliterated perhaps 60 million men,
women, and children in the British Empire. It was often proudly said that
"the sun never sets on the British Empire." In his devastating portrait
of that empire, John Newsinger cites an 1851 quote from Chartist and
socialist Ernest Jones: "On its colonies, the sun never sets, but the blood
never dries." There are many, many millions of lives that were consumed in
the Irish famine, the Opium wars in China, the suppression of the Indian
rebellion of 1857–58, the 1882 invasion of Egypt, in Palestine, in Kenya,
in Malaya, and in so many other places on our planet.[46]

The anticommunist historians are right to point out that the specter
of communism caused some frightened elements to initiate new forms
of violence and terror and murder, designed to ward off "Red Terror" in
Eastern and Central and Southern Europe. But even more, the possibility
of a genuine revolution by the lower classes is what caused upper classes and
procapitalist governments to promote and give considerable support to a
"White Terror." They worked to establish viciously repressive governments
(often animated by extremely antidemocratic and anti-Semitic ideologies)

ringing the new Soviet Republic, from Finland through the Baltic, and
ultimately including portions of the Mediterranean. This was termed by
French prime minister Georges Clemenceau a *cordon sanitaire*, literally a
sanitary barrier, to seal off the "disease" of Bolshevism from the rest of
Europe. This development reached its high point with the fascism that
triumphed in the Italy of Benito Mussolini and the Germany of Adolf
Hitler.[47]

Preliminary to such developments were the dark horrors of World
War I, which Luxemburg saw as the possible beginnings of European
civilization's "downward slide into barbarism." She commented:

> Another such world war and the outlook for socialism will be buried
> beneath the rubble heaped up by imperialist barbarism. This is more
> [significant] than the ruthless destruction of Liege and the Rheims
> cathedral. This is an assault, not on the bourgeois culture of the past,
> but on the socialist culture of the future, a lethal blow against that
> force which carries the future of humanity within itself and which
> alone can bear the precious treasures of the past into a better society.
> Here capitalism lays bare its death's head; here it betrays the fact
> that its historical rationale is used up; its continued domination is no
> longer reconcilable to the progress of humanity.[48]

But, in fact, "another such world war" came in 1939 and continued until
1945. "The legacy of destruction left by World War II is staggering. Eighty
million people were killed, if one includes those who died of starvation
and illness as a result of the war," which is "eight times as many as during
World War I," Ernest Mandel has noted. "Dozens of cities were virtually
totally destroyed, especially in Japan and Germany. Material resources
capable of feeding, clothing, housing, equipping all the poor of this world
were wasted for purely destructive purposes. Forests were torn down and
agricultural land converted into wasteland on a scale not witnessed since
the Thirty Years' War or the Mongol invasion of the Islamic Empire."[49]

TWISTS AND TURNS

We have noted a strong tendency to define imperialism in the most benign
terms, and there is also a more recent tendency to treat it simply as a left-
wing swear word with no serious meaning. Simple definitions might help

us sort through the issues we are exploring. For example, "imperialism" could be said to mean economic expansion beyond the borders of one's country for the purpose of securing markets, raw materials, and investment opportunities. "Colonialism" could be understood as a particular form such imperialism might take, involving military conquest and formal political control. Additional complexities, of course, need to be factored in, yet some scholars have been skittish in their discussions.

In a distinguished 1969 work on imperialism, for example, Heinz Gollwitzer spent the greater portion of his study focusing on noneconomic dimensions of imperialism, emphasizing that "imperialism . . . gave a political and ideological dimension to colonialism, along with a stronger emphasis on prestige than ever before," and that "the idea that the economy of any country must always have been behind its colonial adventures is incorrect; sometimes there was virtually no economic interest at stake at all." Nonetheless, at certain points he found it necessary to state the inconvenient truth. "There is no doubt that the economy in general, banks and entrepreneurs played a leading role in imperialist politics, and that the imperial power of the state was frequently enough employed for the benefit of commercial and banking interests," Gollwitzer acknowledged: "An examination of European social history between 1880 and 1914 shows that imperialism as a political era and high capitalism as an economic era cannot be separated from each other."[50]

Similarly, in his celebratory 1974 history of the British Empire, John Bowle pauses to critique the British liberal J. A. Hobson's 1902 classic, *Imperialism: A Study*, which he notes "would be developed by Lenin" to become "the foundation of the Marxist-Leninist, Stalinist and Maoist theory of colonialism, now of world influence in political warfare."[51] As is the case with Gollwitzer, however, Bowle acknowledges (while noting with conservative disapproval the influx of Liberals and Laborites on the political scene) that there are important economic dimensions to imperialism: "Beneath the thrusting plutocratic world of cosmopolitan finance and privilege and the more anxious world of realistic statesmen in office and of the advisers, who knew the strategic necessities and the precarious balance of power politics, the old Liberal 'little England' tradition went on, kept alive even by Gladstone, and now reinforced by Fabian Socialism and a Labor party hostile to the establishment."[52] Noting the extension of suffrage in the early decades of the twentieth century, he adds (as readers of Orwell already know): "The last and apparently most imposing period of Empire would thus coincide with the advent of total democracy on the island."[53] (By "total democracy" he means extending the right to vote.)

A momentous historical turn, after World War II, involving a wave of national liberation struggles, brought the dissolution of Europe's colonial empires. Many journalists, politicians, and historians represented this as "the end of imperialism," although according to our definition (consistent with the definitions of Luxemburg, Lenin, and some others) this is not the case. The global interplay of politics, economics, and expansionism to benefit the wealthy global minority was destined to persist in new forms. There was a transition from the colonial hegemony of Britain to the noncolonial hegemony of an imperial United States. Economic expansionism, in continuity with the "open door policy" crafted at the dawn of the twentieth century, has generated violent twists and invasive turns in a foreign policy closely related to US business interests.[54] The same can be said for other capitalist powers.

There are, however, a variety of ways to analyze and theorize the specifics. The theoretical approach of Luxemburg—which sees imperialism as involving the capitalist penetration on noncapitalist portions of the globe—is different from the somewhat more open approach developed by Lenin, along with his comrade Nikolai Bukharin, and there are theorizations and analyses influenced by, but different from, theirs— including those of Paul Baran, Paul Sweezy, Harry Magdoff, Samir Amin, and John Bellamy Foster, as well as (from a somewhat different tradition) Alex Callincos. Bringing in a distinctive "world systems" approach is Immanuel Wallerstein.[55] With their own special twist, David Harvey, Riccardo Bellafiore, and other economists continue to use Rosa Luxemburg's economic perspectives to sort through the dark times in the twenty-first century's early decades.[56]

These theorizations hardly cancel each other out. A work of art twists reality in order to squeeze out truths not otherwise seen. The same is true of theory. Some things are emphasized, others minimized, connections between cause and effect are established. But there are always multiple and interactive causes and effects, and an "effect" can turn around and impact upon the "cause" (thereby transforming itself into a new cause that will create an unanticipated effect). Things that are marginalized can end up having central importance. The truth emphasized by the work of art or the theoretical construct may continue to have validity—but multiple theorizations may highlight the complexities.

DEFENDING THE UNSPOILED VERSUS EATING YOUR HEART OUT

We began with Luxemburg's comment that "imperialism is the political expression of the process of the accumulation of capital in its competitive struggle over the unspoiled remainder of the noncapitalist world environment."[57] To accompany this, we find in her prison letters stunning perceptions worthy of the finest of the fictional representations alluded to in this essay.

On a cold winter day, witnessing the violent beating of innocent, laboring oxen by a sadistic wagon driver, she runs to one of the bleeding, brutalized creatures. As she comes close, she sees "an expression on his black face and in his soft, black eyes like an abused child . . . that has been punished and doesn't know why or what for, doesn't know how to get away from this torment or raw violence."[58] At another time, she responds, to a friend's comment about "the special suffering" of the Jews, that "I am just as much concerned with the poor victims on the rubber plantations of Putumayo, the Blacks in Africa with whose corpses the Europeans play catch," and recalls with horror the comments of an eyewitness to an imperialist massacre of natives in the Kalahari desert: "And the death rattles of the dying, the demented cries of those driven mad by thirst faded away in the sublime stillness of eternity."[59] One recalls Orwell's later vision of "a boot stamping on a human face—forever."[60]

The character Winston Smith in the novel *Nineteen Eight-Four*—regarding systematic brutalization and inhumanity—comments: "I understand *how*. I don't understand *why*."[61] Luxemburg seeks to provide a theoretical key:

> The expansionist imperialism of capitalism, the expression of its highest stage of development and its last phase of existence, produces the [following] economic tendencies: it transforms the entire world into the capitalist mode of production; all outmoded, pre-capitalist forms of production and society are swept away; it converts all the world's riches and means of production into capital, the working masses of all zones into wage slaves. In Africa and Asia, from the

northernmost shores to the tip of South America and the South
Seas, the remnant of ancient primitive communist associations,
feudal systems of domination, patriarchal peasant economies,
traditional forms of craftsmanship are annihilated, crushed by
capital; whole peoples are destroyed and ancient cultures flattened.
All are supplanted by profit mongering in its most modern form.[62]

Capitalism's perpetual need to violate that which is unspoiled (in
Luxemburg's theorizations) draws the attention of David Harvey. "The
idea that capitalism must perpetually have something 'outside of itself'
in order to stabilize itself is worthy of scrutiny," he comments, following
on the observation that "the general thrust of any capitalistic logic of
power is not that [non-capitalist] territories should be held back from
capitalist development, but that they should continuously be opened
up." He goes on to remark, "capitalism can either make use of some pre-
existing outside (non-capitalist) social formations or some sector within
capitalism—such as education—that has not yet been proletarianized) or
it can manufacture it."[63]

In recent decades, advanced capitalist economies have sought to
shape the global economy according to their own profiteering needs,
imposing neoliberal austerity programs on the peoples of the world while
maintaining deepened and often lethal inequalities, also waging an
endless "war on terror" perpetrated by a variety of discontented enemies of
this particular world order (some of the enemies motivated by their own
madness and power-lusts). At the same time, however, we have observed
newly modernized and industrialized areas coming to the fore, often in
seeming challenge to the domination of the older powers. "India, Brazil,
Russia, and China could together rewrite the economic geography of
the world along much fairer lines in the twenty-first century," Harvey
commented hopefully in 2010. "They could well signal the emergence of
an 'anti-neo-liberal' power bloc in the world."[64]

Now joined by South Africa, this new nexus has been nicknamed
the BRICS, and while some left-wing analysts express optimism, others
argue this is simply adding a new layer, not qualitatively less exploitative
or oppressive or destructive of human cultures and the environment (that
is, not qualitatively less capitalistic) than the more established capitalist
powers. It has been shown, too, that if a majority of people in the BRICS

countries are raised to the standard of living predominant in the consumer-capitalist United States, the ecology of our planet will be destroyed.[65]

Today, literary representations have increasingly been supplanted by the cinema. The edgy thriller *Syriana* (2005) shows us ruthless machinations of a corporate-capitalist empire that "takes out" a thoughtful, progressive, radical nationalist of an oil-rich country, thereby perpetuating the global exploitation and misery of millions which—in turn, thanks to the absence of revolutionary alternatives—generates suicidal fundamentalist violence. Fast forward to the year 2027 portrayed in the uncompromising *Children of Men* (2007): In the absence of a socialist alternative (protest movements for global justice were not enough), the world has begun its downward slide into barbarism, a vast cemetery, with a proliferation of environmental and political and social disasters. The final enclave of "civilization" is an increasingly authoritarian and exclusionary (anti-immigrant, antirefugee) husk whose inhumanity infects many who struggle against it—but images of Lenin appear, in the midst of religious icons, in an obscure, nurturing haven of those who reach for humanity's future, and hope is placed in far-away "green-peace" scientists who we never actually see. In *The Road* (2009) we observe handfuls of people surviving environmental collapse, with even smaller handfuls striving to remain "the good guys," struggling to endure while resisting the dehumanization and cannibalism that afflicts roaming gangs of Others—though as a despairing wife says, the Others will probably "find us and rape us and kill us and eat us."[66] One thinks of an old poem by Marge Piercy:

> The mouth of empire
> eats onward through the apple of all.
> Armies of brown men
> are roasted into coffee beans,
> are melted into chocolate,
> are pounded into copper.
> Their blood is refined into oil,
> black river oozing rainbows
> of affluence.[67]

The darkness expands outward to envelop all. Luxemburg's urgent plea, that humanity struggle for a life-affirming socialism rather than suffer the downward slide into barbarism, has also found cinematic expression in such films as *Avatar* (2009) and *The Hunger Games* (2012–15). These reflect actual struggles in the real world for a future better than what we seem to face. Yet we have been told "it is easier to imagine the end of the world than to imagine the end of capitalism."[68]

7

CELEBRATING ROSA
LUXEMBURG'S LETTERS

I dedicate this to the vibrant Clara Heyworth (1983–2011).

I want to thank Annelies Laschitza and Peter Hudis, editors of *The Letters of Rosa Luxemburg*, for the very special gift they have helped provide to all of us, beautifully translated by George Shriver. It is good to celebrate this volume of letters and to honor our comrade Rosa Luxemburg.[1]

Rosa Luxemburg was born in 1871 in a Poland divided under German and Russian domination, and she was involved in revolutionary struggles of each country. Born to a cultured and well-to-do Jewish family in Warsaw, she attended the University of Zurich in Switzerland, receiving a doctorate in economics. While still a teenager, she became active in the revolutionary movement, soon rising into the leadership of the Social-Democratic Party of the Kingdom of Poland. Luxemburg's working-class internationalism, however, caused her to move to Germany to play a more substantial role in the massive and influential German Social Democratic Party (the SPD).

Luxemburg's 1899 polemic *Reform or Revolution?* challenged prominent SPD theoretician Eduard Bernstein, who saw Karl Marx's revolutionary approach as no longer relevant and who argued that a piecemeal reform of capitalism could result in a gradual evolution to socialism. Luxemburg warned that this would "paralyze completely the proletarian class struggle," resulting not in the realization of socialism, but only the reform of capitalism. She insisted that "capitalism, as a result of its own inner contradictions, moves toward a point when it will be unbalanced, when it will simply become impossible."[2] Such a crisis would cause its defenders to destroy whatever social reforms and democracy had been won in previous struggles. (This certainly seems true in our own time!) Sooner or later, workers would have to use revolutionary action, Luxemburg insisted, and establish their own political rule to ensure both the political and economic democracy (rule by the people) that she saw as the core of socialism.

Analyzing mass working–class upsurges that swept through Eastern and Central Europe in 1905, Luxemburg believed capitalism periodically would generate spontaneous insurgencies, which should be anticipated, supported, and led by the organized socialist movement. She offered this perspective in her classic work *The Mass Strike: The Political Party and Tthe rade Unions*, insisting that the more cautious trade union and electoral tactics of the SPD were like the labor of Sisyphus (rolling the boulder up a hill, only to have capitalist dynamics push the gains back down again). Only a revolutionary socialist approach, she insisted, would secure permanent gains for the working class.

Aspects of Rosa Luxemburg's story can best be told, perhaps, by referring to one of her most intimate personal connections, which surfaces again and again in her correspondence, over more than a dozen years. It involves her beloved Mimi, with whom she had a complex relationship. As she wrote to one friend: "Mimi is a scoundrel. She leaped at me from the floor and tried to bite me." Mimi was her cat, although not long afterwards, Luxemburg noted, after returning from Poland to Germany: "Mimi showed me she was happy with me right away and has again become high-spirited, comes running to me like a dog and grabs at the train of my dress."[3] Another time she reported: "I get up early, go for a stroll, and have conversations with Mimi. Yesterday evening this is what she did: I was searching all the rooms for her, but she wasn't there. I was getting worried, and then I discovered her in my bed, but she was lying so that the cover was tucked up prettily right under her chin with her head on the pillow exactly the way I lie, and she looked at me calmly and roguishly."[4]

A myth has often been circulated about Luxemburg, that she was hostile to the Russian revolutionary Vladimir Ilyich Lenin. While they sometimes differed on important matters, however, the two liked and respected one another and often were in agreement. In 1911 she wrote: "Yesterday Lenin came, and up to today he has been here four times already. I enjoy talking with him, he's clever and well educated, and has such an ugly mug, the kind I like to look at."[5] Yet Mimi's relationship with the Bolshevik leader reflects something of Luxemburg's own: she writes that Mimi "impressed Lenin tremendously, he said that only in Siberia had he seen such a magnificent creature, that she was a baskii kot—a majestic cat. She also flirted with him, rolled on her back and behaved enticingly toward him, but when he tried to approach her she whacked him with a paw and snarled like a tiger."[6]

Recollections of Mimi helped sustain her during her years of imprisonment during World War I. She wrote to a friend:

> By the way, everything would be much easier to live through if only I would not forget the basic rule I've made for my life: To be kind and good is the main thing! Plainly and simply, to be good— that resolves and unites everything and is better than all cleverness and insistence on "being right." But who is here to remind me of that, since Mimi is not here? At home so many times she knew how to lead me onto the right road with her long, silent look, so that I always had to smother her with kisses . . . and say to her: You're right, being kind and good is the main thing.[7]

Luxemburg was one of the greatest revolutionary theorists of the twentieth century. Indeed, the next two volumes in the English-language *Complete Works of Rosa Luxemburg* will focus on economic writings, which provide some of her most profound contributions to the vast and rich body of Marxist thought. She explains the imperialist expansion that arose out of the accumulation of capital, which became the title of her 1913 masterpiece. In one of her letters, Luxemburg describes her composition of this great work: "Day and night I neither saw nor heard anything as that one problem developed beautifully before my eyes."[8] Even here, however, the process of thinking involved the great revolutionary socialist slowly pacing back and forth, as she herself tells us, "closely observed by Mimi, who lay on the red plush tablecloth, her little paws crossed, her intelligent head following me."[9]

Luxemburg's study *The Accumulation of Capital* provides an economic analysis of imperialism, and it describes capitalism as an incredibly expansive system with dynamics similar to what would later be termed "globalization." In contrast to the views of Lenin, she saw imperialism as not restricted to "the highest stage" of capitalism. Rather, it is something that one finds at its earliest beginnings—in the period of what Marx called "primitive capitalist accumulation."[10] It would continue nonstop, with increasing velocity and violence. She saw this as intertwined with the rise of militarism—leading to World War I and facing humanity with a choice between "socialism or barbarism," as she put it in her "Junius Pamphlet" of 1915.[11]

More than a theorist, writer, and educator, Luxemburg was also an organizer and activist, imprisoned more than once—by Russian authorities in the wake of the 1905 revolutionary upsurge and by German authorities for her uncompromising opposition to World War I. She helped to form the Spartakusbund (the Spartacus League, named after the rebellious leader of Roman slaves), which rallied revolutionary socialists (workers as well as intellectuals) to do what the SPD had ceased to do: oppose war, imperialism, and capitalism. Despite her criticisms regarding the policies of Lenin and Trotsky (particularly around their restrictions of democracy), she was a supporter of their 1917 Bolshevik Revolution in Russia. Shortly before her death, she helped to found the German Communist Party.

In January 1919, against Luxemburg's warnings, some of her comrades became involved in a premature uprising. In the wake of the revolt's suppression, paramilitary groups (which consisted largely of future Nazis) were organized under the name of the Freikorps, systematically rounding up and murdering left-wing "troublemakers." Luxemburg and her close comrade Karl Liebknecht were among the victims. In his fine biography, one of her younger comrades, Paul Frölich, offered the following description:

> Physically she was not cut out for the role of heroine. She was small, and not very well-proportioned. Because of her hip illness in childhood, her walk was ungainly. Her sharp facial features were pronouncedly Jewish—a face indicating unusual boldness and determination. It provoked an immediate response, either repelling or fascinating people. Everyone felt the strength of her personality. In conversation her face reflected the range of her ever-changing impulses and feelings, from earnest meditation to unrestrained joy, from sympathy and kindliness to asperity and sarcasm. . . . Her large, dark and bright eyes dominated her whole face. They were very expressive, at times searching with a penetrating scrutiny, or thoughtful; at times merry or flashing with excitement. . . . To the end of her life she retained a slight Polish accent, but it lent character to her voice and added a special zest to her humor. Because she was

sensitive to the moods of others, she knew when to remain silent and to listen, as well as how to talk about the trivial things of life in a natural, down-to-earth, and spirited way. All this made every private moment with her a special gift.[12]

8

COMIC BOOK ROSA

Kate Evans, *Red Rosa: A Graphic Biography of Rosa Luxemburg*, edited by Paul Buhle. London: Verso Books, 2015, 220 pages, $16.95.

Perhaps a new comic-book superhero is about to take the world by storm, an unlikely Frau Luxemburg, who transforms from a tiny and odd-looking outsider into the almost unstoppable RED ROSA—Revolutionary Scourge of the Oppressors.

Perhaps. But the volume under review is not that. It is a bold graphic ("comic book") representation of the life and ideas—always clever and, in turns cute, highly informative (the book is incredibly well researched), very funny, inspiring, heartbreaking, and very beautiful.

Who was Rosa Luxemburg?

In *Red Rosa: A Graphic Biography of Rosa Luxemburg*, the artist and writer Kate Evans and editor Paul Buhle have produced a magnificent answer. It is by no means the only answer, but it provides, with great originality and flair, distinctive dimensions that, while being true to what we already know about her, help us to see Rosa Luxemburg and imagine the person she was in new ways—a remarkable accomplishment.

It deserves to be understood in a broader context of cultural representations. "Perhaps more than any other Marxist, Rosa Luxemburg has been remembered in various and diverse works of art," is how my friend Helen Scott began our introduction to Luxemburg's selected writings, *Socialism or Barbarism*, going on to specify:

> In lithographs by Conrad Felixmüller and Käthe Kollwitz; poems by Bertolt Brecht and Oskar Kahnel; fiction by Alfred Döblin; film by Margaretha von Trotta; painting by R.B. Kitaj; and more recently in a novel by Jonathan Rabb and music by the British 'post-punk' bands Ludus and The Murder of Rosa Luxemburg. Possibly this

is because although her life was short—she was only 48 when she was killed—she had a profound impact on world history. In fact, thousands gather in Berlin on the anniversary of her death, bringing red carnations to honor her memory.[1]

An artistically rendered Rosa Luxemburg is demanded by the dynamics of what she was. Consider the words of her close friend and comrade Clara Zetkin:

> In Rosa Luxemburg the socialist idea was a dominating and powerful passion of both heart and brain, a truly creative passion which burned ceaselessly. The great task and the overpowering ambition of this astonishing woman was to prepare the way for social revolution, to clear the path of history for Socialism. To experience the revolution, to fight its battles—that was the highest happiness for her. With a will, determination, selflessness and devotion for which words are too weak, she consecrated her whole life and her whole being to Socialism. She gave herself completely to the cause of Socialism, not only in her tragic death, but throughout her whole life, daily and hourly, through the struggles of many years . . . She was the sharp sword, the living flame of revolution.[2]

This is someone we must understand, and only creative and artistic exploration can connect with some of the qualities to which Zetkin alludes. There is obviously something unusual going on here. Great revolutionaries—Karl Marx, for example, or Vladimir Ilyich Lenin—have generally been known by their last names: Marx, Lenin, etc. But when people speak of Rosa Luxemburg, as often as not, it is "Rosa." Some of us at least give her first and last name together, over and over, when we don't do that with Marx or Lenin, so that we can express the intimacy: Rosa.

It is common, too, that she is transformed into what the person who says her name wants her to be. There is more than one Rosa Luxemburg.

I discovered this myself in my late teens, growing up in Cold War America, searching for informative essays in the early 1960s about this woman who (according to my beloved C. Wright Mills) had one foot firmly planted in democracy, the other firmly planted in revolution, and her head very much up in the Marxist clouds of faith in the working class. Bertram D. Wolfe, a one-time revolutionary turned bitter (and widely published) Cold War anticommunist, provided an immensely influential interpretation that minimized most of what she stood for to make her the Rosa of Democracy engaged in mortal combat with the pernicious Totalitarian Lenin. In contrast, a more knowledgeable and honest—and less widely read—essay by Hannah Arendt (produced by someone who had never presumed to be a revolutionary) sought to be truer to what Luxemburg had actually been about. It also emphasized that, whatever their differences, Luxemburg and Lenin were close and were in the same revolutionary camp. For Arendt, however, the most important thing about Luxemburg (not surprisingly for Arendt) was her penetrating mind and her intellectual integrity.

When we turn to the two most substantial biographies in English, we can view Luxemburg through the lens of a passionate and well-informed younger comrade (Paul Frölich) and through the very different lens of a dispassionate and critical-minded scholar (J. P. Nettl). These two Rosas have much in common, although one account is composed by one in the thick of the struggle, the other by one very much removed—and so the different accounts give one a somewhat different sense of this woman. It may be, too, that the gender of the two, and also a certain modesty, caused these biographers to miss certain elements in the story—including personal dynamics to which others (the fiery Marxist-Humanist philosopher Raya Dunayevskaya, as well as another biographer, Elzbieta Ettinger) give greater attention.

Margarethe von Trotta's magnificent film of 1986, *Rosa Luxemburg*, with the striking performance of Barbara Sukowa, powerfully impacted many people's perceptions. Well researched, splendidly produced, beautifully acted—here was Rosa Luxemburg brought to life. And yet it wasn't. Every work of art necessarily distorts the realities it seeks to portray or convey. That is true here; even in the most elemental ways. Sukowa's face and body are not those of Luxemburg, although there are many other visual portrayals of Luxemburg that go more in the direction of what von Trotta and Sukowa present. In some drawings and posters, the proportions of her face are rebalanced, blemishes are airbrushed away, her nose is "fixed," and the facts that she is very short, tiny, with a body that is crooked, are not shown.

In *Red Rosa* we see a Luxemburg closer to the way she looked, with an animated face that can seem, in turn, plain, sometimes even homely, and sometimes luminous, very beautiful. More than once we see her naked body—our own bodies are so essential to our daily existence, and now this is shown to be true of her as well—and the love-making that is so important to many of us is shown to be part of her life as well. In the course of her life there appear to have been at least four lovers, including a couple of significantly younger men, and this is simply integrated, in *Red Rosa*, into a rich life that includes multiple friendships (including that with her cat Mimi), a passionate love of nature, an enjoyment of food, standing on chairs in order to be seen, intensive studies, reading all the time, and writing, writing, writing, the development of theoretical perspectives, working and organizing and debating with comrades in the course of building the revolutionary workers' movement in Poland, Russia, especially Germany, and throughout the world, with time teaching in socialist party schools, and time served in prison, rallies and demonstrations and street battles, reaching for socialism—and being brought down by barbarism and death.

Yet even now, the book shows, she is vibrantly alive in all of the struggles against oppression and the destructiveness of capitalism, all struggles for a better world of the free and the equal.

This is not Rosa Luxemburg, just as none of the representations of her can be. But this remarkable graphic biography will powerfully impact many people's perceptions of who she was. One must reach for more—more biographical and historical information, perhaps, but especially more of what Rosa herself had to say. Some of us who are already engaged with Red Rosa will certainly get much from Kate Evans's achievement. And because there is much truth here, and because it is a fine and entertaining work of art, it is a good place for many to start.

9

ROSA LUXEMBURG FOR OUR OWN TIME: STRUGGLES FOR REFORM AND REVOLUTION IN THE FACE OF CAPITAL ACCUMULATION

Rosa Luxemburg's passionate engagement with life and the struggle for human freedom is reflected in the quality of her revolutionary perspectives, which have great resonance for our own time. In considering those perspectives today, in this age of globalization, of inequality, of economic downturn and mass insurgency,

- one is struck by Luxemburg's clarity regarding the global capital accumulation process as being destructive, irrational, and corrosive in relation to human needs;

- one is struck by Luxemburg's clarity regarding the impossibility of gradually reforming the negative aspects of capitalism out of existence and the necessity of reform struggles being an integral part of a revolutionary strategy for fundamental social transformation;

- one is struck by Luxemburg's clarity regarding the centrality of the working class—the emerging majority in our capitalist-penetrated world—as a vibrant and creative force (despite exploitation and oppression) that is capable, ultimately, of effectively resisting capitalist degradation and bringing into being a better world based on a socially owned, democratically controlled, and humanistically motivated economy.

All of this comes straight from Karl Marx and was as essential to Luxemburg as it is for us today. Working within this framework—whose details are elaborated in the *Communist Manifesto* and *Capital*—Luxemburg made her own distinctive contributions.

These contributions include:

1. her conceptualization of the interplay of the working-class political party, trade unions, and often spontaneous or semi-spontaneous mass action and her alertness, even greater than what we find in Marx and Engels, to problems of routinism, opportunism, bureaucracy, and elitism in the workers' movement;

2. a profound understanding of the centrality of imperialism and militarism to capitalist development and of their devastating impact on diverse world cultures; and

3. an incredibly clear conceptualization of the "socialism or barbarism" choice facing humanity.[1]

To make the best use of Luxemburg's ideas, I think we should avoid glorifying them; we should, instead, see them as brilliant contributions to a collective project of developing and blending theoretical analyses with practical political strategies and tactics for the cause of human liberation. This was centered within the revolutionary wing of the Socialist International, the Second International. Lars Lih, in describing the theoretical and political orientation of Vladimir Ilyich Lenin, has referred to this collective project as "the best of Second International Marxism,"[2] which is an invaluable resource for those of us today who are engaged in the struggle for life and liberation.

It is especially important for us to break out of and move beyond a standard and grossly distorted interpretation prevalent for many years, especially among Stalinists as well as anticommunists, but also among others. This presents Luxemburg's views as contradicting those of Lenin and the tradition associated with his ideas. While there were definitely differences, sometimes strong differences, between these strong-willed revolutionaries, their disagreements are converted into some kind of Battle of the Titans, a sort of cosmic morality play that prevents us from understanding their shared insights and their sometimes divergent insights. Their disagreements often involve incredibly fruitful differences that highlight different facets of complex realities.[3]

They were both in agreement with the proposition that the layer of socialist activists in the working class, as Luxemburg put it, "are the most enlightened, most class-conscious vanguard of the proletariat. They cannot and dare not wait, in a fatalist fashion, with folded arms for the advent of the 'revolutionary situation,' to wait for that which, in every spontaneous peoples' movement falls from the clouds. On the contrary, they.must now, as always, hasten the development of things and endeavor to accelerate events."[4] They both agreed, as Lenin put it, that "the greater the spontaneous upsurge of the masses and the more widespread the movement, the more rapid, incomparably so, the demand for greater consciousness in the theoretical, political and organizational work" of the Marxist movement.[5]

Neither Lenin nor Luxemburg counterposed the struggle for improvements in the here and now to the struggle for socialist revolution. They both agreed with Lenin's comrade and companion, Nadezhda Krupskaya, when she explained that revolutionaries must be "capable of making good use of every legal possibility, of forging ahead and rallying the masses behind them under the most adverse conditions," interlinking struggles for reforms—for example, workplace struggles "for tea service and ventilation"—into revolutionary strategy.[6] They both agreed with Luxemburg's comment that "the daily struggle for reforms, for the amelioration of the condition of the workers within the framework of the existing social order, and for democratic institutions," is part of this perspective, that "the struggle for reforms is its means; the social revolution, its aim."[7] Insistent that the struggle for reforms must be conducted in a way that advances the revolutionary potential of the working class, they both agreed with the German working-class activist Peter Berten (a comrade of Luxemburg's, and one of her students at the school for activists run by the German Social Democratic Party), when he explained to fellow workers: "Only a revolutionary tactic, which always builds on the reality of class conflict and appeals to the elemental power of the masses, can waken the energy, activism, and enthusiasm of the exploited proletariat." Berten added: "What the proletariat possesses, in addition to its chains, is the power that does not disappear through struggle. Rather it grows until it suffices to break the chains."[8]

Luxemburg argued that "only by demanding from capitalist society all that it is capable of granting have we succeeded here and there in obtaining" modest reforms. "It is only our pressure, our pushing the bourgeois reforms to extremes, which squeezes a quarter ounce of 'good will' out of the bourgeoisie." She concluded that "the independent action of the broadest masses, their own political action, mass demonstrations, mass strikes," would not only bring reforms but "sooner or later break forth into a period of revolutionary struggles for state power."[9]

I am certain that Luxemburg, Lenin, and their comrades (if we could bring them into our own world to benefit from their advice) would urge us to do what they were able to do in their own time: bring together socialist perspectives with the actual working-class struggles and movements of our own time, so that each is infused with the other. This is the only way that the cause of the working-class majority and the cause of socialism can hope to move forward to victory. At the same time, they would insist (I think) that there have been immense changes in the global capitalism we face and in the working-class majority to which we belong and that this must be factored into our thought and action. The proletariat of today is larger and more global than ever, encompassing many occupations and situations once not traditionally seen as "working class"—and much of it is far less organized, more vulnerable, more precarious than in years gone by. In many cases, this calls for new tactics and organizing models.[10]

Not that everything has changed. Luxemburg would naturally continue to insist that

> the proletariat cannot be victorious except through democracy, i.e., by giving full effect to democracy and by linking with each step of its struggle democratic demands formulated in the most resolute terms. . . . Basing ourselves on the democracy already achieved, and exposing its incompleteness under capitalism, we demand the overthrow of capitalism, the expropriation of the bourgeoisie, as a necessary basis both for the abolition of the poverty of the masses and for the *complete* and *all-round* institution of *all* democratic reforms.[11]

These are, of course, the words of Lenin in 1915, but this insistence on the inseparable bond between genuine democracy and genuine socialism was repeated incisively by Luxemburg in her 1918 essay "The Russian Revolution," as her Russian comrades stumbled in the midst of horrific difficulties.[12] And these revolutionary-democratic perspectives resonate in our own time, as the power of the wealthy 1 percent bears down so oppressively and destructively, in so many different ways, on the rest of us throughout the world.

There are elements of Luxemburg's analysis in her classic *The Accumulation of Capital* that help to position us to wrestle insightfully with the nature of the system we are struggling to replace with this socialist democracy. There are, I think, certain strengths in Lenin's analysis of capitalism and imperialism that avoid what seem to me certain rigidities in Luxemburg's approach. But both revolutionaries see imperialism as an exploitative, oppressive, and destructive geographic expansion of capitalism, and both hold to the position later pinpointed by Harry Magdoff that "imperialism is not a matter of choice for a capitalist society; it is the way of life of such a society."[13]

Three features especially differentiate the analysis in *The Accumulation of Capital* from the perspectives of other Marxists such as Lenin, Nikolai Bukharin, and Rudolf Hilferding. One is Luxemburg's argument that in order to keep capitalism going, capitalists must expand into "noncapitalist" areas, geographical territories currently outside of the capitalist economic sphere. A second is her conceptualization of imperialism as not restricted to "the highest stage" or "latest stage" of capitalism. Rather, imperialism is something that one finds at the earliest beginnings of capitalism—in the period of what Marx calls "primitive capitalist accumulation"—and which continues nonstop, with increasing and overwhelming reach and velocity, down to the present (although as some critics note, this does not explain "the changes in the foreign policy of the imperialist countries" beginning in the late nineteenth century).[14] A third is her anthropological sensitivity to the impact of capitalist expansion on the rich variety of the world's peoples and cultures that one cannot find in the key works of Hilferding, Lenin, and Bukharin. "Each new colonial expansion is accompanied, as a matter of course, by a relentless battle of capital against the social and economic ties of the natives," she wrote, "who are also forcibly robbed of their means of production and labor power."[15] The destructive impact of all this on the cultures of the world's peoples was emphasized by Luxemburg as by no other Marxist theorist of her time: "The unbridled greed, the acquisitive instinct of accumulation must by its very nature take every advantage of the conditions of the market and can have no thought for the morrow. It is incapable of seeing far enough to recognize the value of the economic monuments of an older civilization."[16]

The voraciousness of the capital accumulation process on which Luxemburg focuses helps us to understand more than the nature of imperialism. David Harvey has recently made a similar point—that, as he puts it, "the notion that capitalism must perpetually have something 'outside of itself' in order to stabilize itself is worthy of scrutiny." A consequence of relentlessly seeking new outlets for surplus capital and of securing cheaper inputs for the accumulation process, Harvey notes, is that "the 'organic relation' between expanded reproduction on the one hand and the often violent dispossession on the other have shaped the historical geography of capitalism."[17]

Capital, Luxemburg wrote, "cannot manage without the natural resources and the labor power of all territories."[18] This is true of *all territories* indeed, including the territories of our bodies, our family life, our friendships, our creative drives, our sexuality, our dreams, and multiple community and social and cultural activities—permeated by noncapitalist dimensions and energies even in global regions where an advanced capitalist economy more and more predominates. This is reflected in voracious drives for "privatization" as well as in rampant consumerism in so-called "advanced" countries. There is also the vast noncapitalist territory that is the natural environment of our planet.

One could argue that working-class pressures and struggles during previous eras of capitalism more or less created relatively "noncapitalist" territories inside the capitalist heartland: public transportation, public libraries, public housing, public education, national health care, social security, and more. The dynamics of the capital accumulation process that Luxemburg and others analyzed have, over the past few decades, inexorably resulted in capitalist invasions and dispossessions of these "noncapitalist territories" within the capitalist heartland. Some of the more recent assaults have been in the name of "austerity" in the midst of the economic downtown, but well before that a neoliberal onslaught was initiated under the leadership of Ronald Reagan, Margaret Thatcher, and others of that type.

In different ways, erosions and corruptions and dispossessions have afflicted other "noncapitalist" territories in the capitalist heartland— including *within* the trade unions and political parties and cultural institutions of so much of the working-class movement that once represented a challenge to and massive pushback against the capital accumulation process.

In his provocative study *Rebel Cities*, David Harvey has suggested a new way of comprehending this capital accumulation process and the class struggle. Utilizing the conception of "the urban commons" as a distinctive noncapitalist territory—encompassing public services and structures (ranging from parks to schools to streets to neighborhoods and more)— Harvey describes the way through which our cities have been perpetually shaped, demolished, rebuilt, and shaped again to advance the capital accumulation process for the profit of the few at the expense of the many. At the same time, he sees elements of a broadly conceived working-class struggle coming together for the purpose of defending the public interest of the majority of the people and, ultimately, of establishing democratic control over the use of society's economic surpluses for the benefit of the many rather than the profit of the few. He adds an essentially revolutionary caveat—which Luxemburg would certainly have insisted upon—that "increasing the share of the surplus under state control will only work if the state itself is both reformed and brought back under popular control."[19]

For this to be meaningful, the power of the few would have to be replaced by the power of the majority of the people, the capitalist state being replaced by the organized political power of organizations and communities representing the working-class majority, making what the *Communist Manifesto* described as "despotic inroads on the rights of property and the conditions of bourgeois production."[20]

While the line of argument presented here may be in the spirit of Luxemburg's rich contributions, however, it does not conform to the theoretical point in *The Accumulation of Capital* that "surplus value cannot be realized by sale to either workers or capitalists" but only to those living in noncapitalist geographical territories.[21] Only by pushing past this theoretical rigidity, I think, can we get closer to the actuality of capitalism that Luxemburg labored to comprehend. And yet, in essential ways she did get it right.

Luxemburg's understanding of the nature of capitalism precludes the possibility of a compromising "live-and-let-live" approach. In the short run, reforms in the present society can and must be struggled for and secured. But in the medium run as well as the long run, the capital accumulation process cannot allow such reforms to endure. The devastations of imperialism and militarism and war that Luxemburg so eloquently described, and the devastations of exploitation and oppression and dispossession in our daily lives, continue to overwhelm our civilization with the palpable threat of a downward slide into barbarism. As we organize our necessary reform struggles in defense of the workplaces and communities and quality of life on our planet, Luxemburg tells us, we must be building mass consciousness and organizational strength that will be capable of bringing an end to the immense devastations of the capital accumulation process.

Such insights and sensibilities remain a vital resource in the struggle for a world in which the free development of each person will be the condition for the free development of all.

10

QUESTIONS AND REFLECTIONS

[This began with an interview with David Muhlmann, conducted in 2009 over the telephone, which appeared—with perhaps complications of translation into French—in *Réconcilier marxisme et démocraie* (Paris, 2010). Andrew Ryder did a translation from the French, and I edited and revised the text. —PLB]

David Muhlmann: Paul, you have been an engaged intellectual in the American workers' movement for decades. You've written and have been heading up a number of publishing projects concerning Rosa Luxemburg: with Helen Scott, writings, under the title *Socialism or Barbarism: Selected Writings of Rosa Luxemburg* (Pluto Press); with Peter Hudis, William Pelz, and others, her *Collected Works*, beginning with a substantial edition of Rosa Luxemburg's letters, translated by George Shriver. Also there is *The International Encyclopedia of Revolution and Protest*, which contains an important essay by you on Rosa Luxemburg.[1] I want to ask you about your analyses of the work of Rosa Luxemburg and your engagement in the context of the United States. What does it mean to be a revolutionary today? Where are the boundaries, and what is the division, between reformism and socialist action, according to you? In Germany, at the time of Rosa Luxemburg and Eduard Bernstein, all of this appeared very evident.

Paul Le Blanc: That's a very interesting question. To respond to it, it's helpful to clarify the country to which we make reference. One can always respond in an abstract manner, but if one wishes to be seriously engaged in political activity, which corresponds to Luxemburg's approach, it's necessary to ask about the specific situation of one or another country and their interdependence. I am very involved with the US situation, which naturally involves many qualitative differences from that of Germany at the end of the 1890s. The situation in the world is also entirely different. One of the fundamental differences concerns the mass socialist movements, which constituted a key factor in Europe at the dawn of the twentieth century and that never existed—at least to the same extent—in the United States. The type of workers' movement within which Luxemburg and Bernstein participated in Germany simply hasn't existed in the United States. That's a key difference.

Eduard Bernstein's articles are remarkable—they read very well, similar to the writings in many liberal and center-left intellectual publications today, all well-informed and very humane in their content. Bernstein could be right at home in the *New York Review of Books* or in the *Times Literary Supplement*, for example. There are many on the left who are similar to Bernstein and who base great hopes on the "reformism" of President Barack Obama. The "Obama phenomenon" certainly has many dimensions, in some ways reflecting some of positive things Bernstein had to say. To some extent, too, such perspectives are reflected, independently of this, in the labor movement.

Rosa Luxemburg represented an uncommon but incredibly relevant perspective, based on a conception of capitalism that is clearly more accurate than that of Bernstein and many intellectuals of the left today. This is, in my view, key: the contemporary relevance of her economic thought, the capital accumulation process cannot allow for a reformist solution. Related to this, the problem that you have raised on the question of the relationship between reform and revolution is crucial for the radical wing of the US left. We find many leftists who have a sectarian approach—which Luxemburg always thoroughly avoided—theoretically counterposing "the revolution" to reform struggles, without worrying very much about what can be done to mobilize, truly and concretely, the masses of workers.

Luxemburg is constantly wrestling with the interplay between the goal and the movement. The interrelation between reform struggles and global revolutionary strategy was at the center of her thought. I think her approach—that the struggle for reforms necessarily must move in a revolutionary direction—is the only one that is viable. Concretely, this means that following the direction taken by Obama, or contemporary social democracy, reformism of one form or another will not resolve the problems that inevitably flow from the accumulation of capital. It's really the great lesson of the contemporary economic crisis.

D. M.: It is true that the absence of socialist politics in the US workers' movement is a constant question for Europeans, since the famous *Why Is There No Socialism in the United States?* by Werner Sombart, in 1906. I want to ask you about the significance of being Luxemburgist in this context. Given the election of Obama, the economic crisis, and the objective of self-determination of the working class that you have already evoked, what is the "Luxemburgist path," and what follows from this?

P. L. B.: First of all, and this might surprise you, I myself am Luxemburgian *and* Leninist. I consider these two currents compatible. This certainly merits a deeper discussion. I can, in any case, tell you how I see things. There is no revolutionary Marxist organization in the United States, in the Luxemburgist or Leninist sense. You can find bits and pieces, but all of them are fragmented and without mass support. Still, it is important to connect with these groupings, because they have the capacity to form revolutionary Marxist cadres. They have a potential for elitism and sectarianism, but they are no less necessary in forming cadres, like those Luxemburg sought to create within the Polish, German, or Russian social democracies of her time, for example.

I think that it is important, then, to relate to these groups, while being clear that none of them constitute the revolutionary party. A revolutionary party in the sense of Luxemburg or Lenin is necessarily a mass workers' party. But this does not come into being spontaneously; it requires that certain ideas are put forward, and that at least partial struggles are waged—helping people to understand events and to realize that they can influence them. This means that it is essential, then, for Marxist activists to prioritize their involvement in social movements—the workers' movement, movements against racial and gender oppression, the antiwar movement, and others. Building such movements and carrying out political education are essential tasks, and the networks and small groupings of Marxist activists can help precisely to develop such abilities among more and more people—the ability to understand political realities and the ability to help change them. Sometimes it is not possible for these movements to win all that they might, but through the struggles to win some reforms, people learn the necessary skills (to organize meetings and events, or to implement strategies), skills that must be learned because they are not innate. In short, Marxists must help people develop such understanding and skills, and they must also develop strategies that will permit the winning of certain victories, at least partially.

Concerning the current situation in the United States, we must recognize the opportunities presented by the victory of Obama and not attack those who supported him, in response to their center-left orientation. Instead, it is necessary to explain to them clearly our vision of reality and, whether they fully share it or not, at the same time to find points of agreement. We can already reach a common understanding, to a certain degree, on the removal of troops from Iraq and Afghanistan. It's necessary to work with these people, to construct united fronts with them and with other organizations they might belong to, around these issues, as well as around the struggle for a more just system of social security, or the defense of unions, which have the possibility of mobilizing people around their interests and immediate concerns, struggles which can be won now. At the same time, it is necessary to work out a political strategy to maintain a certain independence and put pressure on *all* politicians and bourgeois figures, so that these struggles do not privilege, for example, the Democratic Party or the Obama administration.

D. M.: You think that the Obama victory can represent an opportunity for the radical left, if it serves the working class's autonomy and independence of action . . . ?

P. L. B.: I think that the victory of Obama represents a fantastic opportunity. In the short term, it clearly involves the rapprochement of certain leftists here—who are often called *progressives*—and unions within the Democratic Party. On the other hand, his victory raised expectations, which will be bitterly disappointed, because Obama remains a loyal defender of capitalism. This is why we must act and speak politically and critically right now, without waiting. Because, once the liberals of the Democratic Party have failed, we run the risk of the working masses going in search of the other alternatives proposed by the right. Our challenge lies in the ability to offer alternatives to the left.

This will be possible if we function in an intelligent manner and if we are able to develop and articulate our ideas clearly, without diluting them, all while we meet and organize alongside individuals who are politicized and animated by the campaign and victory of Obama. We need to connect with those who have voted for Obama because his left-sounding rhetoric resonated with them. In this way, as they are feeling the impact of the deception, we will be working to build a left-wing alternative, through the social movements, and—even if this takes some time—through a left-wing political party.

D. M.: I would like to return with you to the historical controversies between Lenin and Luxemburg, because I know that you have written and published so much on both of them. You spoke a moment ago of constructing a "political party." Do you think that the controversies between Rosa and Lenin on the subject of democracy in the party are still relevant? You call yourself Luxemburgist and Leninist: Are you for a kind of synthesis?

P. L. B.: For me, there is not any doubt of the relevance of these discussions. They haven't all been translated into English. Two basic texts include the well-known 1904 *Organizational Problems in Russian Social Democracy* by Luxemburg, followed by Lenin's response (which is not as well known but is equally important). Then there is Luxemburg's 1918 essay "The Russian Revolution." Another text from 1906, "Blanquism and Social Democracy," has been translated recently into English.[2] It's a polemic with Plekhanov in which Luxemburg defends the Bolsheviks and Lenin. She says basically: "Maybe there are certain problems with Lenin, but what he says, does, and represents makes sense, and Plekhanov is unjust in his critique of Bolshevism."

This doesn't annul Luxemburg's criticisms or their importance, but it does help to demonstrate that the image of her as fundamentally opposed to Lenin is unfounded. She is closer to Lenin than is commonly understood. They are both revolutionary Marxists; they are both equally trying to build a revolutionary mass party that can overthrow capitalism. Neither one imagines that such an overthrow will be brought about simply through the spontaneous activity of the working classes, although it can be shown that each of these authors are equally convinced of the importance of such activity. In any event, they are close comrades. Sometimes their divergences of opinion are simply the fruit of differences of perception and of context, while other differences are deeper.

I have studied and written on this, taking Luxemburg's text from 1904 as a point of departure. Lars T. Lih's recent book, *Lenin Rediscovered*, which is excellent, shares the view that Luxemburg misrepresents Lenin. Lenin himself wrote a response, which constitutes, in my view, a brilliant defense of his positions. However, I still consider the essay of 1904 as one of the most important writings ever by Luxemburg; it is an excellent essay, if one leaves to one side the polemical distortion, a distortion which Luxemburg partially abandons in 1906. It is an outstanding text, and the positive aspects that can be found there resonate, I believe, with an intelligent and realistic Leninism.

It is the same for the passages of "The Russian Revolution" on democracy. I disagree with what Luxemburg writes on the constituent assembly, dissolved by the Bolsheviks. One could suggest—as have anarchists, certain left-Mensheviks, and the Left-Socialist Revolutionary Party, as well as the Bolsheviks—that the choice at this time was between the soviets (the democratic councils of workers and peasants) or the constituent assembly. I believe that the direction that they took was the best: if political power was to be in the hands of the democratic councils, then the constituent assembly should be dissolved. I am then in disagreement with Luxemburg on this subject, even if this merits debate. In her view, even if the Bolsheviks were right on this, they could have and should have proceeded differently. That's worth discussing.

For me, her defense of freedom and of democracy as being at the core of socialism is fundamental. Lenin and Trotsky and other revolutionaries were arguing that it was necessary to put aside such things on behalf of a more advanced revolutionary approach. One could argue that under the circumstances, as the civil war was starting to shape up, there would necessarily be violations of freedom and democracy—a position which Luxemburg acknowledged might have truth to it. But she still accuses them of adopting harmful theoretical justifications that place obstacles not only to freedom and democracy, but to socialism. I think she was on-target. Her critique must be incorporated into all revolutionary Marxism.

D. M.: You maintain that it is possible to be at the same time Luxemburgist and Leninist, despite this opposition on the question of democracy . . .

P. L. B.: Yes, I think that this is possible. But many points must be made clear. First of all, when you take Luxemburg seriously, and read and absorb her essay on the mass strike and her discourse at the congress of the founding of the German Communist Party, you can see that she truly believed in the existence of a revolutionary vanguard, which had an actual role to play. She knew the necessity of "social-democratic centralism" at the heart of the party; she employed these kinds of terms, which are Leninist as well as Luxemburgist.

At the same time, it is necessary to examine with a critical eye the events of the epoch of war communism in Russia: in my view, Lenin and Trotsky, as gifted as they were, contributed almost fatal errors to the future of Russian socialism. As Hannah Arendt proposed, it is possible that in 1924, at the death of Lenin, all the paths were still open and did not need to degenerate necessarily toward Stalinism; other possibilities existed. But however it turned out, from Lenin's time, the definitive banning of parties and factions in 1921–22, which was meant to be temporary (or at least certain people believed this) strongly contributed to the triumph of bureaucracy and so made impossible the establishment of soviet democracy, of workers democracy. Luxemburg was very clear on this subject, which was not true of Lenin or even Trotsky, at least until the 1930s.

It seems to me then that the majority of Bolsheviks in this period had a blind spot on questions of democracy and civil liberties. There was a truly Bolshevik Workers' Opposition that came into being on these questions, and it was crushed. It is possible to provide a critical examination of this early period—as was done by Victor Serge, for example—from a Bolshevik point of view.[3] I think that this is necessary, when one speaks of "Luxemburgism" and "Leninism."

D. M.: This also poses the question of what to call the social nature of the USSR. We can see in the critique of Bolshevism made by Rosa Luxemburg the sketch of a theorization of Russia as state capitalist, in the sense that was given to it by Pannekoek, Cliff, or Mattick, notably. From that point of view, the distinction between Bolshevism to the east and social democracy to the west loses its pertinence, because it's a matter of two authoritarian forms of the same bourgeois regime, which only vary by the degree of centralization of capital and the state apparatus, and oppose the revolutionary socialist path, that of socialism "from below" and the auto-emancipation of the working class defended by Luxemburg among others. How do you perceive these debates concerning state capitalism?

P. L. B.: To a degree, I understand the theory of state capitalism. I always tried to grasp certain aspects of it, and I am in the process of reading the very helpful work of Marcel van der Linden, *Western Marxism and the Soviet Union*, which discusses "state capitalism" in relation (and contrast) to other critical theories on the nature of the USSR.[4] I have developed very friendly relations with a group that adheres, for the most part, to conceptions of state capitalism, the International Socialist Organization. One of the theoreticians who I admire and respect, and whose writings I helped to republish, is C. L. R. James, who developed the theory of state capitalism with precision.[5] To me, however, this doesn't represent a useful approach to the history of the USSR, precisely because I believe the thesis of Rosa Luxemburg, on accumulation of capital, which she saw as the decisive factor of imperialism. The theory of the accumulation of capital seems to me absolutely accurate, because I see it in operation in the market society and world that surround me.

It's the accumulation of capital that determines the destructive politics, internally and externally, of capitalist society, and the dynamics of capital accumulation are qualitatively different from those that existed in the USSR. One could argue that the system in the USSR was not progressive or even that it was less progressive than capitalism. In any case, I don't think the economic dynamics operated the same way in one society as in the other. The process of the accumulation of capital is the keystone of capitalism, while it's not at the heart of the Soviet system. Trotsky, in *The Revolution Betrayed*, explains very exactly that it's necessary to discern precisely the meaning of the term "capitalist" before considering this or that state. I think that it is misleading to speak of "state capitalism": this isn't useful, it doesn't necessarily aid thinking. The real point is first what we can hope for and do. For example, I don't think that it's possible to claim convincingly that Cuba is state capitalist, but it is important to underline uncompromisingly the serious problems due to the lack of democracy.[6] I know that a large number of those adhering to a "state capitalism" analysis *continue to defend Cuba against American imperialism, while remaining critical of the Cuban political regime.* That is for me the best approach.

D. M.: More globally, what about the process of accumulation of capital today? How can the differences and divergences between Luxemburg and Lenin on imperialism clarify this for us?

P. L. B.: I should emphasize that I am not an economist, which limits my comprehension of this subject and prevents discussion in a detailed manner regarding certain aspects of the analysis made by Luxemburg. This being understood, I can say that her conception of imperialism is central to her critical approach to the second volume of Marx's *Capital*, and I will say that there are two aspects that seem to me worthy of interest in the debate between Luxemburg and Lenin on imperialism. First, Luxemburg's book, *The Accumulation of Capital*, is particularly remarkable in that it offers a profound critique of the impact of imperialism on diverse population groups and diverse regions of the world; the sensibility and the pertinence of her analysis is similar to that of the best cultural anthropologists. This quality is lacking in Lenin, as well as in Hilferding and numerous other Marxists. Second, and this point isn't incompatible with Lenin, her vision of the accumulation of capital as an inexorable and voracious process that is deployed as an imperialist phenomenon seems to me entirely correct.

However, I find Luxemburg more rigid than Lenin on the question of imperialism; this is maybe owing to the fact that she raised some problems based on her criticisms of the second volume of Marx's *Capital*. She most notably claimed that capitalism was forced to extend itself to noncapitalist regions of the world in order to survive, in order to avoid the moment of absolute economic crisis. Lenin didn't say this at all and didn't agree with her on this issue. I think that he was right. For me, it is undeniable that capitalism must continue to extend itself to noncapitalist regions of the world, but it can also develop itself in new spaces; for example, my body is evidently a noncapitalist region of the world, yet various aspects of body and my life are continually permeated by capitalism, which proceeds inexorably by the generation of new needs.

I feel the dynamic of capitalism is much more complex and more supple than Luxemburg represents. The noncapitalist regions of the globe, geographically speaking, have been terribly dominated in the past; this process is still at work, in a certain manner, and it will be in the future. But capital spreads itself at the same time to new domains, to new fields, in capitalist regions. It seems to me that Lenin's approach, which brings out the economic interpenetration of imperialist powers, permits the grasp of this complexity better.

D. M.: Thank you. I would like to revisit a question that we have already approached: the relationship between democracy and socialism. For me, on the political map, we find the essential heritage of Rosa there: socialism can only be inextricably democratic. What do you think? Have the leftist organizations of the United States integrated this conviction?

P. L. B.: First of all, I am in agreement: Democracy is at the heart of socialism, and not only linked to it. Luxemburg was categorical on this subject, just like Lenin, at least during the greater part of his life: we find certain of his writings concerning the path to follow, notably over the course of World War I, where he deals with the national question and insists on the struggle for democracy and on the necessity for the self-organization of the workers' movement, in a nonequivocal and uncompromising way. Democracy cannot be understood as a later fruit of socialism, it is inseparable from the struggle for socialism, which must be the product of the most profound freedom and of an expansive self-activity of the working class—a key notion also basic to Luxemburg's thought in matters of strategy and tactics. The separation of democracy from socialism is one of the most devastating aspects of Stalinism for the movements of the workers and the oppressed. Socialism without democracy is meaningless: this is essential for us.

In the United States, the organized forces of the left are not very numerous, but this conception of socialism as organically, intrinsically democratic, as a factor permitting the real and full implementation of democracy—and not only as the condition of socialism—is largely shared. This is not the case for all: the individuals and the organizations that have been influenced by Stalinism approach socialism from another point of view. This is particularly the case of those who define the Soviet Union and the countries of Eastern Europe as "socialist countries," although for many of us they definitely were not. I suppose that it works the same in Europe.

D. M.: Absolutely. But I add that an interpretation of Leninism exists that is different from yours, as a nondemocratic path. Many people say that for them, Leninists are in fact Stalinists. Do you understand?

P. L. B.: Absolutely. I know that a certain interpretation of Lenin exists, very antidemocratic and elitist . . . But that's certainly not the case with the Leninism of Lenin. Starting from 1918, however, Lenin, Trotsky, and the Bolshevik leaders contributed to a development that reached its fulfillment with Stalinism—but this was certainly not their intention. And this brings us back to Rosa Luxemburg's 1904 critique. I don't think that this Stalinist outcome was inevitable in Leninism, although it carried within it the seeds, the possibility, of Stalinism. It is necessary to combat the Stalinist danger that exists within a certain variety of "Leninism"— creating small authoritarian sects, susceptible, if they were to win power, to evolving into authoritarian governments.

Yet the problem with which Rosa Luxemburg wrestled over decades, which remains unresolved, is particularly crucial for us today: the relationship between Marxist activists and the larger workers' movement, in avoiding what she called "the two dangers": that of "sinking back to the condition of a sect" or that of "becoming a movement of bourgeois social reform." We owe it to Luxemburg, as we owe it to ourselves, to look, with an attentive and critical eye, at all that she wrote, said, or did on this theme, trying to highlight new and useful ideas, with the goal of promoting the development of socialist and workers' movements, a goal that she always championed.

D. M.: Paul, I have a final question, a little out of step. We live in an epoch where the "productive forces," as Marx said, have transformed more and more into "destructive forces" toward nature, of the surrounding environment. The ecological problem linked to capitalism is never approached in classical Marxism; in Trotsky or Lenin, this doesn't appear. By contrast, Luxemburg expresses a very particular sensibility for nature, plants, animals. Do you think that she could serve as the basis for thinking from a socialist point of view on ecological conditions or other questions not directly related to class?

P. L. B.: Yes, if one focuses on ecology, absolutely. She definitely shows this sensibility. It's necessary, however, not to idealize her too much. One only finds this aspect in her letters, it seems to me; I don't think that her fundamental articles treat this theme. This sensibility is a part of her nature and reflects her perspective on life, and it's that which is found in her letters. This is extremely important. But there's not only her: John

Bellamy Foster finds certain passages in Lenin that also have this sense. And it's in August Bebel, too. That's a good thing! Joel Kovel has insisted that Luxemburg and William Morris both present a particular sensibility in this way, which seems to me correct; one can observe this in Morris in his marvelous *News from Nowhere* and, I believe equally in other of his writings. In Luxemburg's letters, and then in her life, this is very visible and constitutes a godsend for those of us who fight for ecology. At the same time, it's necessary to be modest: these elements are implicit in Luxemburg and are not the object of theorization on her part. They merely point in the direction that we must follow.

11

WHY SHOULD WE CARE WHAT
ROSA LUXEMBURG THOUGHT?

Rosa Luxemburg was a passionate tribune of socialism, penetrating
Marxist theorist and educator whose luminous prose has inspired
millions, revolutionary activist martyr. What are we to make of her now?

In *The Marxists*, C. Wright Mills wrote that Luxemburg "occupied
a peculiar, and powerless, position between the Second and the Third
Internationals." Because she was "passionately for democracy and for
freedom in all of the decisive meanings of those terms," Mills explains,
and because this was fused "in her belief in the revolutionary spontaneity
of the proletarian masses," she should be seen as having one foot in the
Socialist International, the other foot in the Communist International,
"and her head, I am afraid, in the cloudier, more utopian reaches of classic
Marxism."[1] If someone was so disconnected from the hard realities of her
own time, why should one care what she might have thought about the
complexities of ours?

Hannah Arendt's marvelous essay on Rosa tells us that Luxemburg has
been so important to so many because after her death she became "a symbol
of nostalgia for the good old times of the movement, when hopes were
green, the revolution around the corner, and, most important, the faith
in the capacities of the masses and in the moral integrity of the Socialist
or Communist leadership was still intact."[2] Arendt adds that "it speaks
not only for the person of Rosa Luxemburg, but also for the qualities
of the older generation of the left, that the legend—vague, confused,
inaccurate in nearly all details—could spread throughout the world and
come to life whenever a 'New Left' sprang into being."[3] But she concludes
by insisting on the continuing relevance of Luxemburg's actual ideas,
expressing the hope "that she will finally find her place in the education

of political scientists in the countries of the West" (and presumably the East, the North, the South), since—according to Luxemburg's biographer J. P. Nettl, whom she quoted—"her ideas belong wherever the history of political ideas is seriously taught."[4]

Stephen Eric Bronner, it seems clear, inclines very much toward this view. And he seems admirably determined not to allow what is valid in Luxemburg's thought and life to get lost in the clouds of utopianism or the fog of nostalgia.

I have not read enough of Bronner's writings. His small book on Rosa Luxemburg is not bad, though I differ with some of the interpretation. (For me, no one has matched Rosa's comrade Paul Frölich's classic biography of her.) I have read Bronner's edition of Rosa Luxemburg's letters, which is incredibly fine, and while Luxemburg may deserve most of the credit for that, I feel genuine gratitude for Bronner's valuable selections, editing, notes, and introductory essay. And I have read his warm and illuminating essay on his teacher Henry Pachter, a very thoughtful one-time follower of Luxemburg who passed through Communism to the social-democracy of Irving Howe's *Dissent*.[5]

But after reading his self-defense in response to the criticisms of Alan Johnson and David Camfield, I will certainly want to look at the other works Bronner mentions throughout his footnotes—*Socialism Unbound*, *Moments of Decision*, *Ideas in Action*, and others. First of all, because here is an intelligence that is wonderfully steeped in the Marxist tradition and the history of the socialist movement. But it is also an intelligence so obviously humane, alert, and critical that one is compelled (if the reader is to do justice to himself or herself) to open one's mind in a manner that undermines dogmatic interpretations of valued beliefs. This is so even if one differs with the author's conclusions.

This is why I liked his essay "Red Dreams and the New Millennium: Notes on the Legacy of Rosa Luxemburg."[6] It constituted a genuine challenge for us to consider the contemporary relevance of Luxemburg, and it truly helped to bring her alive. I think she herself would not have accepted important aspects and assumptions of the argument. But I liked it. Because what is more important than what Rosa Luxemburg would have thought of Bronner's essay is the extent to which it identifies real issues and real problems facing us. She lived and wrote and acted in a context in which mass working-class movements throughout Europe were animated by socialist ideas and history crackled with revolutionary possibilities. It is silly to allow ourselves the daydream— when we read her words or think about her life—that this defines our own reality. So what *is* Rosa's legacy for us? Good question!

THE DEBATE...AND THE STAKES

And then in the next issue of *New Politics*, thanks to Johnson and Camfield, there were not one but two critiques—twenty pages of critique to the original six pages of Bronner's talk—defending Luxemburg's revolutionary Marxism against the revisionist offender. The critiques were comradely in tone, as Bronner acknowledged in his seventeen-page rejoinder that (in a comradely tone) lambasted his critics.[7]

Why on earth would I be wandering into this debate on Rosa Luxemburg?

In part, the answer is that I want to help these people stop fighting. It seems to me the comrades are (to a certain extent) arguing past each other: too much learning, too much knowledge, too many fine-turned phrases getting in the way of identifying what's really what in the world and how they see the world. It isn't clear to me to what extent—in life, in practical politics—they actually disagree.

In part, the answer is that they are differing over more than the legacy of Rosa Luxemburg. A little bit in his first contribution but somewhat more in his second, Bronner seems to raise issues having to do with the continuing relevance of Marxism and the possibility of socialism. Since so much of my own life has been animated by a belief in such relevance and such a possibility, I find myself drawn to the debate like a moth to a nighttime porch light. Especially since a majority of those who used to think the way I did now seem not to. This is hardly the first time.

Once upon a time, I belonged to a relatively small would-be revolutionary party that was in trouble. It was larger than any would-be revolutionary group existing in the United States today, and the trouble it was in was that, despite some very good work it had done (in part, *because* of some very good work it had done), it was sinking under the weight of its own unrealistic expectations. There was full freedom of discussion in the organization and the right to dissent from the party leadership, but (especially under the circumstances) anyone who seriously made use of those rights risked, at the very least, undermining his or her position as a respected comrade. What's worse, at a certain point the party leadership decided (in a manner neither open nor honest) to replace one set of party dogmas with another set of party dogmas. There were many contradictions, many confusions, many foolish and wrong things being said and done. I would sit in meetings, wanting to continue making my own modest contributions to the revolutionary party and remain everyone's friend, gritting my teeth, saying to myself: "Don't be a fool, don't say anything, don't go looking for trouble, don't say anything, let it go, don't say anything . . . ." And then like a fool I would open my mouth and disagree with the majority position.

Nor is my problem simply still agreeing with Luxemburg. The majority dogma among radicals today, for example, is certainly what Bronner writes: "Leninism is as dead as a doornail everywhere other than among the sects that are reminiscent of antagonistic amoeba fighting each other to the death in a drop of water."[8] Good heavens! And here I am, still considering myself a Leninist. What an embarrassment. But this may be as good a place as any to explain myself. I still consider myself a Leninist because, in large measure, I consider authentic Leninism to include a commitment to the following propositions:

- Capitalism is inherently a vicious, exploitative, oppressive, dehumanizing system that should be replaced with socialism— rule by the people over the economy, the free development of each being the condition for the free development of all.

- In modern capitalist society it is the working class (not simply "factory workers," but all those individuals and their families dependent on the sale of one's ability to work for a paycheck) that is in the process of becoming a majority class and potentially has the power to bring great changes.

- Socialism and the working class must be merged if the possibility of the one and the potential of the other, and the triumph of both, are to be realized.

- Mass struggles for reforms that advance economic justice and democratic rights are necessary in and of themselves but are also important as the basis for a serious struggle for socialism—both because this is a training ground for working-class activists capable of making socialism a reality, and because capitalism ultimately is incapable of providing actual economic justice and genuine democracy.

- Under modern-day capitalism, the state—even in the form of the more or less *democratic republic*—necessarily reflects, and is necessarily structured to reflect, the power and the needs of the capitalist economy and of the most powerful sectors of the capitalist class. Partial gains for the workers and oppressed must be fought for and can sometimes be secured within that context, but a genuinely democratic republic that truly reflects the needs and power of the working-class majority will require a fundamental restructuring—a radical democratization—of the structure of the state.

- From the very beginning, capitalism was expansive and global—seeking markets, raw materials, and investment opportunities regardless of national and other boundaries—and this aggressive expansionism is intertwined with the policies and structures of the modern-day state, constituting the imperialism of our time: often peaceful when possible, but murderous when necessary, often expressed with the rhetoric and gestures of profound humanitarianism, but always shaped to harmonize with the ability of capitalist power elites to overcome all impediments to the maximization of their profits.

- Just as capitalism is a global system, so is the exploitation of those who labor throughout the world an international reality, which means that the workers of all countries and regions, instead of competing against one another, need to work together. Such working-class internationalism will mean the mutual strengthening—through shared experiences and insights—of working-class liberation forces in each country, and victories in one sector of the world will, quite substantially and materially, make possible victories in other parts of the world for workers and oppressed people.

- The politically advanced, activist layers of the working class (the vanguard), must organize themselves into a coherent socialist organization, a party that is democratic but also disciplined, that—with its leaflets, newspapers and other literature, its study circles and mass meetings, its demonstrations and trade union efforts, its reform struggles and election campaigns, and ultimately its mass mobilizations and confrontations with the powers that be—will be capable of accumulating and sharing with more and more workers a blend of practical political experience and the knowledge and analyses associated with Marxism, ultimately helping the working class to take political power.

• Socialism will not be brought about simply through the slow and steady gathering together of an electoral and parliamentary majority. A powerful majority capable of establishing working-class political power and the socialist reconstruction of society can only be forged through militant, dynamic, revolutionary struggles that will confront and overcome capitalist power structures in the workplaces, the communities, and the political arena.

A couple of points can be made here. One is that this is not just Leninism. There is ample material to demonstrate (including my own books, *From Marx to Gramsci, Lenin and the Revolutionary Party, Rosa Luxemburg: Reflections and Writings*) that the perspectives outlined above are hardly the exclusive property of Lenin.[9] They were broadly accepted (more or less) by all in the revolutionary Marxist tradition, starting with Marx and Engels themselves, also embracing Trotsky and Gramsci, and certainly including Luxemburg. One could add that Luxemburg's thought also contains vitally important criticisms of Lenin's practice, criticisms that are essential for any revolutionary socialism, including Leninism, which seeks to learn from the mistakes of revolutionary socialists. But Luxemburg and Lenin saw themselves, and they remain, partisans of the same set of commitments.

Yet simply because all the holy names in the revolutionary Marxist pantheon said that something is true, does that make it true? Maybe it *was* true once long ago when these people were still alive. Does that make it true now? This is precisely Bronner's challenge to us.

CAPITALISM, THE STATE, AND IMPERIALISM

Which brings me to my second point. We should care what Rosa Luxemburg thought because so much of her thought continues to be relevant to the capitalist realities in which we find ourselves enmeshed. Setting aside this rhetorical flourish and that overly optimistic or pessimistic error, the basic critique of capitalism—economically, socially, politically—still holds up all too well.

That is why I have a problem with some of the key assertions in Bronner's challenge. In his second article he tells us that "a liberal republic" structured along the lines of the United States "must serve as the precondition for socialism." He asserts that "not the institutional structures of liberal-democratic states, but rather the elites within those states, erect barriers to addressing exploitation, oppression, and ecological destruction."[10] I am not in favor of our simply turning our backs on the "bourgeois-democratic" state. To the extent that it is democratic, that is a precious acquisition for all of us, and especially for the working class, and we should struggle for reforms within that context. But we should not blind ourselves to the fact that "the Founding Fathers" (and all of the politically powerful "fathers" who have come since) really did—quite consciously—structure the American Republic in order to protect and advance the interests of the market economy and of those who possess great wealth and property. It is wrong for Bronner, in the name of going beyond Marxist dogma, to pretend that this isn't so.

Worse, in his first article he says this: "The only institutions capable of furthering internationalism are now intertwined with capitalist interests and they tend to privilege strong states over their weaker brethren. But I think Luxemburg would have realized that the choice between furthering relatively progressive ends through imperfect institutions and not intervening in order to forestall genocide in Rwanda or Sierra Leone is self-evident."[11]

It is important to look at the actual history of the world over the past hundred years to avoid making naive mistakes. There have been many imperialist military interventions that principled socialists have actively opposed, from the Spanish-American War and the invasion of the Philippines, to World War I, to US intervention in Vietnam, to the various interventions in Central America and the Caribbean, to the bombing of innocents in Afghanistan. On the other hand, it can be argued that there are other military interventions against which it would have been wrong to mobilize. A classic case was the US war effort against Nazi Germany in World War II. One could, perhaps, identify other possible examples in recent times.

But there is a difference between not organizing an antiwar movement and actually mobilizing for war. Should one give political support to interventions by (or advocate interventions to be carried out by) what is essentially an imperialist war machine? Historians William Appleman Williams, Gabriel Kolko, Lloyd Gardner, and Walter LaFeber have demonstrated that US foreign policy in 1941–45 was inseparable from the imperial commitment to "the Open Door Policy" and to establishing "the American Century" at the expense of the world's peoples. It should be clear that imperialist "humanitarianism" will certainly be a pretext for the primary goal: maintaining an imperialist world order in which, for example, the richest 20 percent of the world's population receives 82.7 percent of the total world income, the world's 225 richest people have a combined income that is equal to the combined annual income of the world's 2.5 billion poorest people, and 40,000 of the world's children die of malnutrition each day.

Bronner is wrong to speculate that the Rosa Luxemburg we know would have agreed with his support of certain imperialist interventions. It was alien to all that she said, all that she did, all that she was. That hardly settles the matter. It is not important that Rosa Luxemburg would have disagreed with Stephen Eric Bronner if all that shows us is her inability to transcend her revolutionary socialist "dogmatism." (Of course, I think she would have been not dogmatic but simply right.)

What is most surprising and disheartening about Bronner's response to his critics is the way that the final paragraphs of his rejoinder seem to rise in a crescendo of far-reaching innuendo which seems to question not only revolutionary socialism but perhaps socialism as such, and he consigns Johnson and Camfield (representing "a tiny minority . . . to whom no one ever listens") to the junk heap of history.[12] That's not very helpful, and it undercuts the genuine contribution that he has to offer.

THE WORKING CLASS AND SOCIALISM ... AND
OUR OWN STRUGGLES FOR A BETTER WORLD

In approaching Bronner's genuine contribution, it may be useful to remind ourselves of the two points made earlier about our beloved Rosa: (a) there is a broadly defined revolutionary socialist tradition with Luxemburg gloriously and luminously in the thick of it, and (b) essential aspects of the analysis associated with that revolutionary socialist tradition continue to make sense for our own time. But there is a third point that must be made. And it brings us to what strikes me as the most valid and important aspect of Bronner's challenge.

If we still lived in the golden age of classical Marxism or the heroic years of revolutionary Communism, with massive workers' movements characterized by significant levels of class consciousness, there would be obvious ways to make the revolutionary Marxist orientation relevant to the political struggles of our time. But those are not our realities, as Bronner brutally insists over and over. "The industrial working class is on the wane, and the labor movement is no longer what it once was. . . . The proletarian internationals of the past have collapsed." Yes, absolutely true. "The question facing the left is whether to embrace outmoded forms of thinking or provide new meaning for an old vision." Yes, absolutely true. "Internationalist, socialist, and democratic principles must be adapted to meet new historical conditions without surrendering their bite." Yes, absolutely true. One might say (Bronner might not, but I would) that the Marxist analysis of capitalism remains powerful, while the perspective of revolutionary working-class struggle for socialism is in shambles. As Bronner puts it: "the power of capital still rests on the degree of *organizational* and *ideological* disunity among workers."[13]

So what *is* to be done?

Despite a tone of self-assurance that Bronner sometimes employs (a tone that so many of us tend toward, even—or especially—when we are unsure), his suggested paths "forward" seem to go in different and contradictory directions. Some of them seem to demand a relentless honesty and critical-mindedness (in regard to Marxist verities), others seem to suspend critical thinking and indulge in self-deception (in regard to the nature of the state and imperialism). We have seen that some of his thoughts seem to throw into question the revolutionary socialist goal as such. Others take us in the direction of continuing struggle in the spirit of Rosa Luxemburg. In what follows, I want to trace precisely those elements, which one can find in the articles of Bronner and of his two critics.

"A more radical commitment to social justice must now increasingly seek new forms of alliance between workers and members of the new social movements,"[14] according to Bronner, and Alan Johnson fully agrees, adding that the precondition of independent working-class politics involves "the political constitution of the multi-ethnic and gendered working class as a unity-in-difference."[15]

In the words of David Camfield, we need "a socialist political strategy which takes as its start-point struggles, however small, in which working-class and oppressed people assert their needs against employers, governments and other instances of domination," emphasizing the need for "unions and community-based workers organizations (including those of women and other oppressed people)," as well as "organizations of peasants, indigenous people, students, and others,"[16] adding up to an inclusiveness that also characterizes the vision of Bronner and Johnson.

"Justice is a river with many tributaries," Bronner tells us. "Most women and gays, minorities and environmentalists, have a stake in protecting the gains made by labor in the past as surely as labor had a stake in furthering many of their concerns in the future."[17] Johnson tells us of the need (also explicitly embraced by the others) to "fight to protect threatened welfare benefits and democratic rights from roll-back, and then to use that resistance as a springboard to fight for further reforms is a key to socialist advance."[18] All of them identify with movements for global justice associated with massive international protests in Seattle, Prague, Washington, Genoa, and elsewhere.

These are the kinds of things that we should all work on, in as serious and as organized a manner as possible, with the relatively small socialist groups finding ways to work in alliance rather than sectarian competition. In fact, most of the people in the diverse, fragmented, incohesive working-class majority don't identify with any of the existing groups, and it is most important to reach out to these brothers and sisters who will be new to the struggle and are not about to enlist in one or another ideological group. We cannot afford to pretend that we are living in the glory days of either the Second International or Third International—in many ways our organizational and ideological realities are closer to those preceding the First International. And of course in some ways they are very different from anything that has come before.

It seems to me that the basic elements of the revolutionary socialist tradition still make sense, but there are ways to apply them that would make very little sense. Times are different. Just as aspects of the *Communist Manifesto* made more sense in 1890 and 1930 than they did in 1848, so will aspects of the revolutionary socialist perspective have greater relevance later than they do now (especially if we do the right kinds of things between now and then). We should have respect for our history, but not at the expense of respecting, understanding, and being able to truly affect the present-day realities of which we are part. We need tools, not totems or artifacts.

With modesty and patience, as we help advance the struggles for a better world and learn from the experiences associated with these struggles, we may be able to sort more adequately through the divergent notions of Bronner and his critics. And then what Rosa Luxemburg and her comrades thought may take on a greater meaning than we are able to find at this particular moment in history.

(2002)

12

A HUNDRED YEARS AFTER HER DEATH

Ten years after the murder of Rosa Luxemburg in January 1919, playwright and poet Bertolt Brecht wrote in his typically stark, homely verse:

> Red Rosa now has vanished too.
> Where she lies is hid from view.
> She told the poor what life's about.
> And so now the rich have rubbed her out.[1]

Luxemburg was born in 1871, in a Poland divided under German and Russian domination, and she played a role in the working-class socialist movement of each country.

Yet her influence has been global. She was part of a mass working-class movement seeking a transition from capitalism to socialism. The decades following her death saw increasing crises and finally a half-century decline and collapse of that movement.

But triumphant capitalism has (by its very nature, Luxemburg would tell us) generated a growing discontent and socialist renewal, giving new relevance to what Luxemburg thought and did and tried to do.

THE QUALITY OF HER THOUGHT AND LIFE

Luxemburg's Marxism denied that "economic development rushes headlong, like an autonomous locomotive on the tracks of history, and that politics, ideology, etc. are content to toddle behind like forsaken, passive freight wagons."[2]

Her passion was unusual among theoreticians of the socialist movement. "Unrelenting revolutionary activity coupled with boundless humanity—that alone is the real life-giving force of socialism," she wrote amid crashing empires and working-class insurgency after World War I.[3]

Joining the massive Social Democratic Party of Germany in the 1890s, she explained to a Polish friend: "I do not agree with the view that it is foolish to be an idealist in the German movement."[4]

Noting that idealistic impulses permeated the movement, she added that "the ultimate principle" in all of her revolutionary activity was "to remain true to myself without regard for the surroundings and the others—thus, I am and will remain an idealist in the German as well as the Polish movement."[5]

Luxemburg's blend of critical-minded social science and humanistic idealism was matched by activism, from the time she was a teenager to the moment of her death.

She wrote articles, essays, pamphlets, and books. She lectured at a socialist party school educating activist cadres and at meetings of workers in various cities and towns of Germany and Poland, with eloquent speeches at mass rallies.

Luxemburg also worked with comrades—openly and legally when possible, in the revolutionary underground when necessary—to develop effective organizations, strategies and tactics, in workplaces and in the streets, to challenge the capitalist status quo. For this, she was imprisoned more than once—and finally murdered by a reactionary death squad.

According to one comrade, Max Adler, "an untamed revolutionary force was alive in this frail little woman. It was characteristic of her, however, that her intellect never lost control of her temperament, so that the revolutionary fire with which she always spoke was also mingled with coolheaded reflectiveness, and the effect of this fire was not destructive but warming and illuminating."[6]

Luxemburg's student and biographer Paul Frölich remembered "large, dark and bright eyes . . . very expressive, at times searching with a penetrating scrutiny, or thoughtful; at times merry and flashing with excitement. They reflected an ever-alert intellect and an indomitable soul." Her slight Polish accent "lent character to her voice and added a special zest to her humor . . . All this made every private moment with her a special gift."[7]

Private life was also animated by passionate engagement—her deepest friendships within a substantial circle of women, comradeship, and (in a few cases) love relationships among a select number of men.

Especially vibrant was a connection with Mimi, her imperious cat. We find in her writings powerful traces of attention to and appreciation for multiple creatures (birds, oxen, insects), not to mention plants and multiple manifestations of the natural world. Her environmental sensibilities are particularly relevant to the troubling realities of today.

REFORM, MASS ACTION, AND REVOLUTION

Insights can be gained by considering Luxemburg's interactions with other prominent theoreticians of the mass socialist workers' movement when the twenty-five-year-old moved to Germany: Eduard Bernstein and Karl Kautsky.

An opportunistic variant of trade unionism and a vote-getting electoral fixation had become prevalent in the movement's organizational apparatus. This bureaucratic conservatism was reflected in an approach developed by Bernstein.

The traditional approach, grounded in the *Communist Manifesto* by Karl Marx and Friedrich Engels, called for masses of workers to struggle for improvements within capitalist society, learning how to defend their rights and confront capitalism.

"Between social reforms and revolution there exists for the Social Democracy an indissoluble tie," Luxemburg explained. "The struggle for reforms is its means; the social revolution, its aim."[8]

Bernstein revised this, arguing for piling up reforms without a revolution, enabling socialists to collaborate as partners in progress with liberal-minded capitalists for a gradual evolution to socialism.

This was incredibly naïve, Luxemburg insisted. The violence-prone capitalist elite would not willingly give up its power, and the dynamics of the capitalist economy would not allow for such a painless transition. Bernstein's orientation would transform the German Social Democratic Party from a socialist party into "a movement of bourgeois social reform."[9]

Capitalist dynamics periodically generated crises that jolted semi-spontaneous upsurges, Luxemburg concluded, based on insurgent explosions of 1905 in Russia. She vividly described "the whirlwind and the storm" and "the fire and glow of the mass strike and the street fighting."[10]

This would not necessarily result in socialist revolution, she felt, but could become "the starting point of a feverish work of organization" that would embrace more of the working class, enabling it to fight for reforms in a manner that would help prepare it for the revolutionary struggle.[11]

She believed "the most enlightened, most class-conscious vanguard of the proletariat" in Germany, Poland, Russia, and elsewhere should play an essential role in this process.[12]

Initially, her friend and prominent Marxist cothinker Karl Kautsky had stood with Luxemburg in rejecting Bernstein's revisionism. Yet pressures of the social democratic and trade union bureaucracy made him retreat into an increasingly rigid (but also diluted) Marxist "orthodoxy." By 1910, he worked to marginalize Luxemburg's revolutionary orientation within the German Social Democratic Party.

Kautsky's political compromises with more conservative elements in his party were not simply inconsistent with the spirit of Marx or Luxemburg. No less than Bernstein, he was failing to prepare the working class for tumultuous crises and violence inherent in the nature of capitalism. Luxemburg's take on capitalism can be found in her 1913 classic *The Accumulation of Capital*.

THE ACCUMULATION OF CAPITAL

Luxemburg embraced Marx's stricture to "doubt everything"—including daring to question and disagree with some of what Marx himself had to say.

In her economic analysis, Luxemburg criticized the second volume of Marx's *Capital*, which she considered an underdeveloped and incomplete aspect of Marx's analysis of how surplus value is realized. Focusing on the global dynamics of the capitalist system, she saw imperialism as being at the heart of capitalist development.

Capitalism is an expansive system driven by the dynamic of accumulation. Capital in the form of money is invested in capital in the form of raw materials, tools, and labor-power, which is transformed—by the squeezing of actual labor out of the labor-power of the workers—into capital in the form of the commodities thereby produced, whose increased value is realized through the sale of the commodities for more money than was originally invested.

The capitalists extract their profits from this increased capital, only to be driven to invest more capital in order to achieve ever-greater capital accumulation.

Capitalism's global expansion, Luxemburg emphasized, aggressively coexists in a world of different cultures, different types of society, and different modes of production—that is, different economic systems. Imperialism exists at the earliest beginnings of capitalism and continues nonstop, with increasing and overwhelming reach and velocity, down to the present.

Distinctive to Luxemburg's contribution is her anthropological sensitivity to the impact of capitalist expansion on the rich variety of the world's peoples and cultures: the destruction of the English peasants and artisans; the destruction of the Indians or Native American peoples; the enslavement of African peoples by the European powers; the ruination of small farmers in the midwestern and western regions of the United States; the onslaught of French colonialism in Algeria; the onslaught of British colonialism in India; British incursions into China, with special reference to the Opium wars; and the onslaught of British colonialism in South Africa. (She made lengthy reference to the three-way struggle of Black African peoples, the Dutch Boers and the British.)

No less dramatic is Luxemburg's perception of the economic role of militarism in the globalization of the market economy. "Militarism fulfills a quite definite function in the history of capital, accompanying as it does every historical phase of accumulation," she commented, noting that it was decisive in subordinating portions of the world to exploitation by capitalist enterprise.[13]

It played an explosive role in rivalry between competing imperialist powers. More than this, military spending "is in itself a province of accumulation," making the modern state a primary "buyer for the mass of products containing the capitalized surplus value," she wrote—although through taxes, "the workers foot the bill."[14]

SOCIALISM OR BARBARISM

The violence and inhumanity visited on those victimized by imperialist oppression in "faraway lands" of Asia and Africa became a murderous backdraft which exploded into Europe with the imperialist slaughter of 1914–18: World War I.

Luxemburg concluded that humanity stood at a crossroads—either forward to socialism or a downward slide into barbarism.[15] She was horrified that a majority of social democratic leaders, in Germany and most other countries, ended up going along with their various countries' war efforts. Others who, like Luxemburg, remained true to their revolutionary socialist principles were arrested and imprisoned.

She and her comrades in the newly formed Spartacus League—expelled from the German Social Democratic Party and soon to become the German Communist Party—warned: "The beast of capital that conjured up the hell of the world war is not capable of banishing it again, of restoring real order, of insuring bread and work, peace and civilization, and justice and liberty to tortured humanity."[16]

There were like-minded comrades around the world—and in Russia, some of these were able to lead a successful revolution in 1917. As Luxemburg wrote in celebration of the revolution: "All the revolutionary honor and capacity which western Social-Democracy lacked was represented by the Bolsheviks. Their October uprising was not only the actual salvation of the Russian Revolution; it was also the salvation of the honor of international socialism . . . Whatever a party could offer of courage, revolutionary farsightedness and consistency in an historic hour, Lenin, Trotsky and all the other comrades have given in good measure."[17]

Yet she was critical of the Bolsheviks' glorification of authoritarian practices when confronted with a brutal civil war.

"Socialist democracy is not something which begins only in the promised land after the foundations of socialist economy are created," she argued. "It does not come as some sort of Christmas present for the worthy people who, in the interim, have loyally supported a handful of socialist dictators."[18]

Luxemburg insisted that the best way to help the Russian Revolution remain true to its initial democratic and socialist ideals was for other workers' movements to end their Russian comrades' terrible isolation by making revolutions in their own countries.

But revolutionary hopes and possibilities in Germany were betrayed by opportunistic, deal-making social democratic leaders, who supported the repression and murder of revolutionaries like Luxemburg.

Capitalist elites ultimately backed the fascism of Mussolini and Hitler, whose grim qualities were matched—thanks to revolutionary Russia's isolation—by the Stalin dictatorship's barbaric corruption of the communist movement. A second and even more devastating world war engulfed the planet, followed by decades of instability, violence, and cultural and environmental degradation.

Yet amid what some have perceived as a downward slide into barbarism, many have continued to be inspired by the last words Red Rosa wrote: "Tomorrow the revolution . . . will proclaim with trumpets blazing: I was, I am, I shall be."[19]

NOTES

INTRODUCTION

1. C. Wright Mills, *The Marxists* (New York: Dell, 1977).
2. Bertram D. Wolfe, *Strange Communists I Have Known* (New York: Stein and Day, 1982).
3. Hannah Arendt, "A Heroine of Revolution," *New York Review of Books*, October 6, 1966.
4. Rosa Luxemburg, *The Mass Strike: The Political Party and the Trade Unions, and the Junius Pamphlet* (New York: Harper & Row, 1971).
5. Paul Le Blanc, *Unfinished Leninism: The Rise and Return of a Revolutionary Doctrine* (Chicago: Haymarket Books, 2014).
6. Rosa Luxemburg, *The Letters of Rosa Luxemburg*, in *Complete Works of Rosa Luxemburg*, edited by Peter Hudis, Annelies Laschitza, and Georg Adler, translated by George Shriver (London: Verso, 2011).
7. David Muhlmann, *Réconcilier marxism et démocratie* (Paris: Éditions du Seuil, 2010).
8. Jason Schulman, ed., *Rosa Luxemburg: Her Life and Legacy* (New York: Palgrave Macmillan, 2013).

ROSA LUXEMBURG (1871–1919)

1. Both works appear in Rosa Luxemburg, *Rosa Luxemburg Speaks*, edited by Mary-Alice Waters (New York: Pathfinder Press, 1970).
2. Rosa Luxemburg, "Reform or Revolution?" in *Rosa Luxemburg Speaks*, 76–78, 80, 87, 90.
3. Luxemburg, "Reform," 39, 81.
4. Rosa Luxemburg, "Organizational Question of Social Democracy," in *Rosa Luxemburg Speaks*, 129.
5. Rosa Luxemburg, "Progress and Stagnation in Marxism," in *Rosa Luxemburg Speaks*, 111.
6. Karl Marx, *Capital*, vol. 1 (New York: Vintage Books, 1977), 874–926; Karl Marx, *Grundrisse: Foundations of the Critique of Political Economy, Rough Draft* (Harmondsworth, UK: Penguin Books, 1973), 459–71. This is termed "original accumulation" or "previous accumulation" by some scholars and theorists.
7. Rosa Luxemburg, *The Accumulation of Capital* (London: Routledge, Kegan and Paul, 1951), 364–65, 452–53. For a revised understanding of this matter, see Paul

Le Blanc, "Introduction: Rosa Luxemburg and the Global Violence of Capitalism," in *The Complete Works of Rosa Luxemburg, Vol. 2: Economic Writings*, edited by Peter Hudis and Paul Le Blanc (London: Verso, 2015), xv–xvi.

8. Luxemburg, *The Accumulation of Capital*, 455.

9. Rosa Luxemburg, "The Mass Strike, the Political Party, and the Trade Unions," in *Rosa Luxemburg Speaks*, 214.

10. Luxemburg, "Mass Strike," 192–93.

11. Luxemburg, "Mass Strike," 176, 192, 194, 200.

12. Luxemburg, "The Russian Revolution," in *Rosa Luxemburg Speaks*, 374.

13. Luxemburg, "The Russian Revolution," 389–91.

14. Luxemburg, "The Russian Revolution," 389.

15. Luxemburg, "The Russian Revolution," 391.

16. Rosa Luxemburg, "Junius Pamphlet: The Crisis in the German Social Democracy" in *Rosa Luxemburg Speaks*, 269.

REVOLUTIONARY MIND AND SPIRIT

1. Quoted in Raya Dunayevskaya, *Rosa Luxemburg, Women's Liberation, and Marx's Philosophy of Revolution* (Atlantic Highlands, NJ: Humanities Press, 1981), 90.

2. Hannah Arendt, "Rosa Luxemburg, 1871–1919," in *Men in Dark Times* (New York: Harcourt, Brace and World, 1968), 45–47.

3. Dunayevskaya, *Rosa Luxemburg, Women's Liberation, and Marx's Philosophy of Revolution*, 92.

4. Dunayevskaya, *Luxemburg, Women's Liberation*, 92, 93.

5. Stephen Eric Bronner, ed., *The Letters of Rosa Luxemburg*, New Edition (Atlantic Highlands, NJ: Humanities Press, 1993), 163.

6. Bronner, *The Letters of Rosa Luxemburg*, 60.

7. Quoted in Paul Frölich, *Rosa Luxemburg: Her Life and Work*, translated by Johanna Hoornweg (New York: Monthly Review Press, 1972), 189.

8. Bronner, *The Letters of Rosa Luxemburg*, 60, 77–78.

9. Bronner, *The Letters of Rosa Luxemburg*, 75.

10. Bronner, *The Letters of Rosa Luxemburg*, 94–95.

11. Bronner, *The Letters of Rosa Luxemburg*, 95.

12. Gary P. Steenson, *"Not One Man! Not One Penny!" German Social Democracy, 1863–1914* (Pittsburgh: University of Pittsburgh Press, 1981), 221.

13. John Moses, "Socialist Trade Unionism in Imperial Germany, 1871–1914," in *Bernstein to Brandt, A Short History of German Social Democracy*, ed. Roger Fletcher (London: Edward Arnold, 1987), 31.

14. Richard N. Hunt, *German Social Democracy, 1918–1933* (Chicago: Quadrangle, 1970), 166.

15. Hunt, *German Social Democracy*, 59.

16. Hunt, *German Social Democracy*, 59,

17. The classic work on this development is Carl Schorske, *German Social Democracy*,

1905–1917 (Cambridge: Harvard University Press, 1955).

18. Bronner, *The Letters of Rosa Luxemburg,* 121.

19. Schorske, *German Social Democracy, 1905–1917,* 181.

20. Bronner, *The Letters of Rosa Luxemburg,* 149.

21. Bronner, *The Letters of Rosa Luxemburg,* 179.

22. Bronner, *The Letters of Rosa Luxemburg,* 294.

23. Bronner, *The Letters of Rosa Luxemburg,* 295.

24. Quoted in Frölich, *Rosa Luxemburg,* 39–40.

25. Bronner, *The Letters of Rosa Luxemburg,* 185.

26. Bronner, *The Letters of Rosa Luxemburg, 185.*

27. Bronner, *The Letters of Rosa Luxemburg,* 204.

28. Bronner, *The Letters of Rosa Luxemburg, 204.*

29. Frölich, *Rosa Luxemburg,* 197.

30. Frölich, *Rosa Luxemburg,* 182.

31. Frölich, *Rosa Luxemburg,* 173.

32. Frölich, *Rosa Luxemburg,* 179.

33. Frölich, *Rosa Luxemburg,* 179–180.

34. "Spartacus Manifesto," in Anton Kaes, Martin Jay, and Edward Dimendberg, eds., *The Weimar Sourcebook* (Berkeley: University of California Press, 1994), 38.

35. The slogans are commonly associated with US President Woodrow Wilson's justification for leading the United States into World War I. His speech to Congress on a declaration of war against Germany (April 2, 1917) asserted: "The world must be made safe for democracy. Its peace must be planted upon the tested foundations of liberty." See Louis M. Hacker and Hélène S. Zahler, eds., *The Shaping of the American Tradition* (New York: Columbia University Press, 1947), 1006. Many studies document that things turned out quite differently—as indicated in the summary provided in Louis L. Snyder, *The World in the Twentieth Century,* rev. ed. (New York: D. Van Nostrand, 1964), 28–36.

LUXEMBURG AND THE GERMAN LABOR MOVEMENT

1. The "dual revolution" concept is highlighted in Eric Hobsbawm, *The Age of Revolution, 1789–1848* (New York: Vintage Books, 1996), and a succinct survey of the rise, within this context, of the workers' movement of which Luxemburg was part is provided in Wolfgang Abendroth, *A Short History of the European Working Class* (New York: Monthly Review Press, 1972). For a useful new collection of Luxemburg's writings, see Peter Hudis and Keven B. Anderson, eds., *The Rosa Luxemburg Reader* (New York: Monthly Review Press, 2004), which, in combination with volumes edited by Paul Le Blanc and Mary-Alice Waters cited below, provides the bulk of what is available to English-language readers.

2. Quoted by Richard Hyman, "Marxism and the Sociology of Trade Unionism," in *Trade Unions under Capitalism,* edited by Tom Clarke and Laurie Clements (Glasgow: Fontana, 1977), 389. The range of Luxemburg's thought, and key

aspects of her biography and personality, are elaborated in Paul Le Blanc, ed., *Rosa Luxemburg, Reflections and Writings* (Amherst, NY: Humanity Books, 1999), which on pp. 256–57 includes a somewhat different translation of this passage from Luxemburg's "Speech to the Founding Convention of the Communist Party."

3. Mary Nolan, *Social Democracy and Society: Working-Class Radicalism in Dusseldorf, 1890–1920* (Cambridge: Cambridge University Press, 1981). Other works that do this include Vernon Lidtke, *The Alternative Culture: Socialist Labor in Imperial Germany* (New York: Oxford University Press, 1985), and William Pelz, *The Spartakusbund and the German Working Class Movement, 1914–1919* (Lewiston, NY: Edwin Mellen Press, 1987).

4. The fundamental continuity in the orientation of Marx and Luxemburg (along with Engels, Lenin, Trotsky, and Gramsci) is indicated in Paul Le Blanc, *From Marx to Gramsci: A Reader in Revolutionary Marxist Politics* (Chicago: Haymarket Books, 2016).

5. Le Blanc, *From Marx to Gramsci*, 102, 131.

6. Le Blanc, *From Marx to Gramsci*, 99, 108, 135–37, 162, 191, 216.

7. Le Blanc, *From Marx to Gramsci*, 127.

8. Rosa Luxemburg, "Organizational Question of Social Democracy," in *Rosa Luxemburg Speaks*, edited by Mary-Alice Waters (New York: Pathfinder Press, 1970), 128–29.

9. Carl Schorske, *German Social Democracy, 1905–1917* (New York: John Wiley and Sons, 1955).

10. Paul Frölich, *Rosa Luxemburg: Her Life and Work* (New York: Monthly Review Press, 1972), 146–47.

11. Peter Nettl, *Rosa Luxemburg*, abr. ed. (New York: Oxford University Press, 1969), 264. Also see Norman Geras, *The Legacy of Rosa Luxemburg* (London: Verso, 1983).

12. Eisner's comments can be found in Rosa Luxemburg, "Speech to Nuremberg Congress (1908)," in *Selected Political Writings*, edited by Dick Howard (New York: Monthly Review Press, 1971), 281.

13. Luxemburg, "Speech to Nuremburg Congress (1908)," 281–82.

14. Nolan, *Social Democracy and Society*, 187, 189, 193–95, 233, 243.

15. Nolan, *Social Democracy and Society*, 243.

16. Luxemburg, "The Mass Strike, the Political Party, and the Trade Unions," in *Rosa Luxemburg Speaks*, 176, 192, 194.

17. Luxemburg, "The Mass Strike," 214–15.

18. Luxemburg, "The Idea of May Day on the March," in *Selected Political Writings*, 319–21.

19. Stephen Eric Bronner, ed., *The Letters of Rosa Luxemburg*, New Edition (Atlantic Highlands, NJ: Humanities Press, 1993), 75, 121.

20. Pelz, *The Spartakusbund and the German Working Class Movement, 1914–1919*, 286.

21. Pelz, *Spartakusbund and the German Working Class*, 287, 289. Also valuable,

although evaluating Luxemburg and the *Spartakusbund* more critically, is Chris Harman, *The Lost Revolution, Germany 1918–1923* (London: Bookmarks, 1982).

LUXEMBURG AND LENIN ON REVOLUTIONARY ORGANIZATION

1. For a full political biography of Lenin, the following three volumes read in sequence are recommended: Leon Trotsky, *The Young Lenin* (Garden City, NJ: Doubleday, 1972); N. K. Krupskaya, *Reminiscences of Lenin* (New York: International Publishers, 1970); Moshe Lewin, *Lenin's Last Struggle* (New York: Vintage Books, 1970). The best political biography of Rosa Luxemburg remains that of her comrade Paul Frölich, *Rosa Luxemburg: Her Life and Work* (New York: Monthly Review Press, 1972), but also see Norman Geras, *The Legacy of Rosa Luxemburg* (London: Verso, 1983).

2. Franz Borkenau, *World Communism* (Ann Arbor: University of Michigan Press, 1962), 45, 141.

3. Max Shachtman, "Lenin and Luxemburg," *New International* 4, no. 5 (May 1938): 144.

4. Max Nomad, *Aspects of Revolt* (New York: Noonday Press, 1961), 264.

5. Ernest Mandel, letter to author, May 14, 1986.

6. Peter Nettl, *Rosa Luxemburg* (London: Oxford University Press, 1969), 344, 353.

7. Robert Blobaum, *Feliks Dzierzynski and the SDKPiL: A Study of the Origins of Polish Communism* (New York: Columbia University Press, 1994), 4.

8. Blobaum, *Feliks Dzierzynski*, 4.

9. Blobaum, *Feliks Dzierzynski*, 103.

10. Nettl, *Rosa Luxemburg*, 181.

11. Blobaum, *Feliks Dzierzynski and the SDKPiL*, 89, 104.

12. Blobaum, *Feliks Dzierzynski*, 85, 254n74.

13. Blobaum, *Feliks Dzierzynski*, 112–13.

14. Blobaum, *Feliks Dzierzynski*, 201.

15. Blobaum, *Feliks Dzierzynski*, 231.

16. Blobaum, *Feliks Dzierzynski*, 150–51, 226–27.

17. Blobaum, *Feliks Dzierzynski*, 203.

18. Blobaum, *Feliks Dzierzynski*, 205–8.

19. Rosa Luxemburg, *Selected Political Writings*, edited by Dick Howard (New York: Monthly Review Press, 1971), 283.

20. Shachtman, "Lenin and Luxemburg," 143.

21. Rosa Luxemburg, *Rosa Luxemburg Speaks*, edited by Mary-Alice Waters (New York: Pathfinder Press, 1970), 128–29.

22. Luxemburg, *Rosa Luxemburg Speaks*, 128–29.

23. Neil Harding, *Lenin's Political Thought*, vol. 1 (New York: St. Martin's Press, 1975), 195.

24. Krupskaya, *Reminiscences of Lenin*, 94.

25. V. I. Lenin, *Collected Works*, vol. 34 (Moscow: Progress Publishers, 1960–1970), 161–62, 165.

26. Lenin, *Collected Works*, vol. 34, 166 (emphasis in original).

27. Krupskaya, *Reminiscences of Lenin*, 89.

28. Harding, *Lenin's Political Thought*, 193–94.

29. Krupskaya, *Reminiscences of Lenin*, 96.

30. Lenin, *Collected Works*, vol. 34, 161 (emphasis in original).

31. This comes through even in the pro-Menshevik account by Israel Getzler, *Marrov: A Political Biography of a Russian Social Democrat* (Cambridge: Cambridge University Press, 1967); see 83, 88–89.

32. Lenin, *Collected Works*, vol. 7, 472.

33. Luxemburg, *Rosa Luxemburg Speaks*, 116.

34. Lenin, *Collected Works*, vol. 7, 472–73.

35. Luxemburg, *Rosa Luxemburg Speaks*, 118.

36. Lenin, *Collected Works*, vol. 7, 473–74.

37. Lenin, *Collected Works*, 474.

38. Luxemburg, *Rosa Luxemburg Speaks*, 119.

39. Lenin, *Collected Works*, vol. 7, 474.

40. Luxemburg, *Rosa Luxemburg Speaks*, 117, 119.

41. Lenin, *Collected Works*, vol. 7, 474–75.

42. Luxemburg, *Rosa Luxemburg Speaks*, 119, 122.

43. Luxemburg, *Rosa Luxemburg Speaks*, 200.

44. Luxemburg, *Rosa Luxemburg Speaks*, 374.

45. Luxemburg, *Rosa Luxemburg Speaks*, 375.

46. Brian Pearce, ed., *1903, Second Congress of the Russian Social Democratic Labour Party, Complete Text of the Minutes* (London: New Park, 1978), 312, 328.

47. Lenin, *Selected Works*, vol. 1 (New York: International Publishers, 1967), 312,

48. Lenin, *Selected Works*, 306 (emphasis in original).

49. Luxemburg, *Rosa Luxemburg Speaks*, 119.

50. Luxemburg, *Rosa Luxemburg Speaks*, 118, 129.

51. Luxemburg, *Rosa Luxemburg Speaks*, 129–30.

52. See Solomon Schwarz, *The Russian Revolution of 1905: The Workers' Movement and the Formation of Bolshevism and Menshevism* (Chicago: University of Chicago Press, 1967), and Marcel Liebman, "Lenin in 1905: A Revolution That Shook a Doctrine," *Monthly Review* 21, no. 11 (April 1970).

53. Lenin, *Collected Works*, vol. 10, 33–34, 314.

54. Krupskaya, *Reminiscences of Lenin*, 167.

55. Gregory Zinoviev, *History of the Bolshevik Party* (London: New Park, 1973), 153–54.

56. See Leopold H. Haimson, "The Problem of Social Stability in Urban Russia, 1905–1917," *Slavic Review* 23, no. 4 (December 1964): 619–42, and 24, no. 1 (March 1965): 1–22; Ronald Grigor Suny, "Toward a Social History of the October Revolution," *American Historical Review* 88, no. 1 (February 1983): 31–52.

57. Blobaum, *Feliks Dzierzynski and the SDKPiL*, 145–46, 148, 217–19, 228–29.

58. See Carl Schorske, *German Social Democracy*, 1905–1917 (Cambridge, MA: Harvard University Press, 1955), and Frölich, *Rosa Luxemburg*.

59. Shachtman, "Lenin and Luxemburg," 144.

60. Michael Löwy, "Rosa Luxemburg's Conception of Socialism or Barbarism," *Bulletin in Defense of Marxism*, no. 26 (January 1986): 15. For details, see Helmut Trotnow, *Karl Liebknecht: A Political Biography* (Hamden, CT: Archon Books, 1984), 165–68, 174.

61. On the US scene, see Paul Le Blanc, "The Tragedy of American Communism," *Michigan Quarterly Review* 21, no. 3 (Summer 1982); James O'Brien, "American Leninism in the 1970s," *Radical America* 11, no. 6 (November 1977–February 1978); John Trinkl, "Where Have All the Party Builders Gone?" *Guardian*, August 21, September 4, September 11, 1985; Cliff Connor, *Crisis in the Socialist Workers Party* (New York: F. I. T., 1984).

THE CHALLENGE OF REVOLUTIONARY DEMOCRACY

1. An exploration of the Marxist tradition, and in part of Luxemburg's place within it, is offered in Paul Le Blanc, *From Marx to Gramsci: A Reader in the Revolutionary Marxist Politics* (Atlantic Highlands, NJ: Humanities Press, 1996), with further elaboration in Paul Le Blanc, *Rosa Luxemburg: Reflections and Writings* (Amherst, NY: Humanity Books, 1999). Key texts on this and related matters are Paul Frölich, *Rosa Luxemburg: Her Life and Work* (New York: Monthly Review, 1972) and Norman Geras, *The Legacy of Rosa Luxemburg* (London: Verso, 1983). The English-language anthology of Luxemburg's writings is also well worth consulting: *The Rosa Luxemburg Reader*, edited by Peter Hudis and Kevin B. Anderson (New York: Monthly Review Press, 2004).

2. Quoted in Wendy Forrest, *Rosa Luxemburg* (London: Hamish Hamilton, 1989), 61.

3. See, for example, Rosa Luxemburg, "What Is Economics?" in *Rosa Luxemburg Speaks*, edited by Mary-Alice Waters (New York: Pathfinder Press, 1970), 220–49.

4. Relevant here are Arno J. Mayer, *The Persistence of the Old Regime: Europe to the Great War* (New York: Pantheon Books, 1981), and Peter Nettl, *Rosa Luxemburg*, abr. ed. (New York: Oxford University Press, 1969), 72–74, 304–5.

5. The centrality of democracy in Marxism has been well-established for some time. See, for example, Michael Löwy, *The Theory of Revolution in the Young Marx* (Chicago: Haymarket Books, 2005); Richard N. Hunt, *The Political Ideas of Marx and Engels*, 2 vols. (Pittsburgh: University of Pittsburgh Press, 1974, 1984); and August H. Nimtz, Jr., *Marx and Engels, Their Contribution to the Democratic Breakthrough* (Albany: New York State University Press, 2000). On the centrality of Marxist-influenced political movements for the advance of democracy, see Dietrich Rueschemeyer, Evelyne Huber Stephens, and John D. Stephens, *Capitalist Development and Democracy* (Chicago: University of Chicago Press, 1992), and Geoff Eley, *Forging Democracy: The History of the Left in Europe, 1850–2000* (New

York: Oxford University Press, 2002).

6. Rosa Luxemburg, *The Accumulation of Capital* (London: Routledge and Kegan Paul, 1951), and "The Junius Pamphlet: The Crisis and the German Social Democracy," in *Rosa Luxemburg Speaks*, 261–331.

7. Karl Marx and Frederick Engels, "Manifesto of the Communist Party," in Le Blanc, *From Marx to Gramsci*, 143; Vladimir Ilyich Lenin, "The State and Revolution," in *Selected Works*, vol. 2 (New York: International Publishers, 1967), 343–45.

8. Luxemburg, "The Russian Revolution," in *Rosa Luxemburg Speaks*, 389.

9. Luxemburg, "The Russian Revolution," 391.

10. The points on sausages and Sisyphus can be found in Luxemburg's "Reform or Revolution," in *Rosa Luxemburg Speaks*, 71, 77. Her growing critique of the orientation of the social-democratic leadership can be seen in "The Mass Strike, the Political Party, and the Trade Unions" in *Rosa Luxemburg Speaks*, 155–218, in the excerpt of "Theory and Practice" in Le Blanc, *Rosa Luxemburg*, 139–74 (a slightly different excerpt is in *The Rosa Luxemburg Reader*, 208–31), and correspondence is to be found in Stephen Eric Bronner, ed., *The Letters of Rosa Luxemburg*, 2d ed. (Atlantic Highlands, NJ: Humanities Press, 1993), 129, 149, 179, 294–95.

11. See Carl Schorske, *German Social Democracy 1905–1917: The Development of the Great Schism* (New York: Wiley, 1955).

12. These perspectives are elaborated in sources cited in Endnote 9 as well as in Luxemburg's "Speech to the Founding Convention of the German Communist Party" in *Rosa Luxemburg Speaks*, 405–27.

13. Luxemburg, "The Russian Revolution" in *Rosa Luxemburg Speaks*, 374.

14. Luxemburg, "The Russian Revolution," 389–91. Also see "The Socialization of Society," in *The Rosa Luxemburg Reader*, 346–48.

15. One recent effort pushing in this direction is the late Daniel Singer's final work, *Whose Millennium? Theirs or Ours?* (New York: Monthly Review Press, 1999). Another can be found in materials by Eveline Wittich, Paul Le Blanc, Ottakar Luban, Thomas Deve, and Lindsey Collen in a conference of scholars and activists organized by South Africa's Anti-War Movement and the Johannesburg office of the Rosa Luxemburg Foundation: *Militarism and War: Rosa Luxemburg Political Education Seminar 2004* (Johannesburg, South Africa: Khanya College Publishing, 2005).

HEART OF DARKNESS

1. Rosa Luxemburg, *The Accumulation of Capital*, in *The Complete Works of Rosa Luxemburg*, vol. 2, edited by Peter Hudis and Paul Le Blanc (London: Verso Books, 2015), 325.

2. Luxemburg, *The Accumulation of Capital,*, 6.

3. Chinua Achebe, "An Image of Africa: Racism in Conrad's *Heart of Darkness*," and Edward Saïd, "Two Visions in *Heart of Darkness*," in Paul B. Armstrong, ed., *Heart of Darkness, Norton Critical Edition* (New York: W. W. Norton, 2006), 337, 423.

4. Achebe, "Image of Africa," in *Heart of Darkness*, Norton Critical Edition, 344, 348.

5. Conrad, *"Heart of Darkness,"* in *Heart of Darkness*, Norton Critical Edition, 50, 69.

6. Conrad, *Heart of Darkness*, Norton Critical Edition, 73–76.

7. Jonah Raskin, *The Mythology of Imperialism: A Revolutionary Critique of British Literature and Society in the Modern Age* (New York: Monthly Review Press, 2009), 44, 153.

8. Rosa Luxemburg, "The Crisis of German Social Democracy," in Paul Le Blanc and Helen C. Scott, eds., *Socialism or Barbarism: The Selected Writings of Rosa Luxemburg* (London: Pluto Press, 2010), 210.

9. Luxemburg, *The Accumulation of Capital*, in *The Complete Works of Rosa Luxemburg*, vol. 2, 325.

10. James Joll, *The Origins of the First World War* (London and New York: Longman, 1984), 127, 148, 152–53.

11. Richard Toye, *Churchill's Empire: The World That Made Him and the World He Made* (New York: St. Martin's Griffin, 2011), 93, 95.

12. Clive Ponting, *Churchill* (London: Sinclair-Stevenson, 1994), 132.

13. W. E. B. Du Bois, *The World and Africa* (New York: International Publishers, 1965), 23.

14. Hannah Arendt, *The Origins of Totalitarianism*, New Edition (New York: Harcourt, Brace & World, 1966), 185.

15. Arendt, *Origins of Totalitarianism*. See also a thoughtful analysis of Arendt's work in Dominico Losurdo, "Towards a Critique of the Category of Totalitarianism," *Historical Materialism* 12, no. 2 (2004): 23–55.

16. Luxemburg, *The Accumulation of Capital*, 267.

17. Luxemburg, *The Accumulation of Capital*, 267.

18. Luxemburg, *The Accumulation of Capital*, 270.

19. Luxemburg, "The Crisis of German Social Democracy," 204.

20. John Bowle, *The Imperial Achievement: The Rise and Transformation of the British Empire* (Harmondsworth, England: Penguin Books, 1977), 14, 514.

21. Bowle, *The Imperial Achievement*, 553.

22. Bowle, *The Imperial Achievement*, 554–56.

23. From articles by Bernstein in H. Tudor and J. M. Tudor, eds., *Marxism and Social Democracy: The Revisionist Controversy 1896–1898* (Cambridge, UK: Cambridge University Press, 1988), 52–53, 67, 153, 168–69.

24. Bernstein, *Marxism and Social Democracy*, 169; John Riddell, ed., *Lenin's Struggle for a Revolutionary International, Documents: 1907–1916, The Preparatory Years* (New York: Monad Press/Pathfinder Press, 1984), 10–11.

25. See Peter Gay, *The Dilemma of Democratic Socialism: Eduard Bernstein's Challenge to Marx* (New York: Collier Books, 1962); Bernard Semmel, *Imperialism and Social Reform: English Social-Imperial Thought 1895–1914* (Garden City, NY: Anchor/Doubleday, 1968); Wolfgang J. Mommsen, *Max Weber and German Politics, 1890–1920* (Chicago: University of Chicago Press, 1990), 68–90, 112; and Richard Bellamy, "Liberalism and Nationalism in the Thought of Max Weber,"

History of European Ideas 14, no. 4 (1992): 499–507.

26. Karl Kautsky, "Imperialism" and "Nation State, Imperialist State, and Confederation," in *Discovering Imperialism: Social Democracy to World War I*, edited and translated by Richard B. Day and Daniel Gaido (Chicago: Haymarket Books, 2012), 757, 806, 811.

27. Kautsky, "Imperialism," 758.

28. Kautsky, "Nation State, Imperialist State, and Confederation," 806, 811; Patrick Goode, ed., *Karl Kautsky, Selected Political Writings* (New York: St. Martin's Press, 1983), 91–92.

29. George Lichtheim, *Imperialism* (New York: Praeger, 1971); Michael Harrington, *Toward a Democratic Left* (Baltimore, MD: Penguin Books, 1969), 86–218.

30. George Orwell, *The Road to Wigan Pier* (Harmondsworth, England: Penguin, 1962), 126–28.

31. George Orwell, "Rudyard Kipling," in *Essays, Journalism and Letters, Vol.1: My Country Right or Left 1940–43*, edited by Sonia Orwell and Ian Angus (Boston: David R. Godine, 2000), 186.

32. Orwell, "Rudyard Kipling," 186.

33. Orwell, "Rudyard Kipling," 187.

34. George Woodcock, *The Crystal Spirit: A Study of George Orwell* (New York: Schocken Books, 1984), 83–84. A nasty critique of Orwell is offered in Raskin, *The Mythology of Imperialism*, 69–74, but see John Newsinger, *Orwell's Politics* (New York: Palgrave Macmillan, 2001).

35. The magnificent fictional works by Melville and Twain are widely available. See also Janet Smith, ed., *Mark Twain on the Damned Human Race* (New York: Hill and Wang, 1994), and F. O. Matthiessen, *American Renaissance: Art and Expression in the Age of Emerson and Whitman* (London: Oxford University Press, 1941).

36. Rosa Luxemburg, "The Idea of May Day on the March," in *Selected Writings of Rosa Luxemburg*, edited by Dick Howard (New York: Monthly Review Press, 1971), 320–21.

37. This passage is taken from the editor's commentary in V. I. Lenin, *Revolution, Democracy, Socialism: Selected Writings*, edited by Paul Le Blanc (London: Pluto Press, 2008), 216; information is drawn from Louis L. Snyder, *The World in the Twentieth Century* (Princeton, NJ: D. Van Nostrand, 1964), 35. See also Marc Ferro, *The Great War 1914–1918* (London: Routledge and Kegan Paul, 1973).

38. Lenin, "The Historical Destiny of the Doctrine of Karl Marx," in *Revolution, Democracy, Socialism*, 221.

39. Gorter is quoted in Paul Le Blanc, *Lenin and the Revolutionary Party* (Chicago: Haymarket Books, 2015), 214; R. Craig Nelson, *War on War: Lenin, the Zimmerwald Left, and the Origins of the Communist International* (Chicago: Haymarket Books, 2009), 49–50.

40. Bowle, *The Imperial Achievement*, 496.

41. Paul Frölich, *Rosa Luxemburg* (Chicago: Haymarket Books, 2010), 285–87, 293–301; J. P. Nettl, *Rosa Luxemburg*, vol. 2 (London: Oxford University Press, 1966), 768–78.

42. Mommsen, *Max Weber and German Politics, 1890–1920*, 305; Bellamy, "Liberal-

ism and Nationalism in the Thought of Max Weber," 502–3; Peter Breiner, *Max Weber and Democratic Politics* (Ithaca, NY: Cornell University Press, 1996), 180; Kieran Allen, *Max Weber: A Critical Introduction* (London: Pluto, 2004), 15–31, 154–72.

43. Roderick Stackelberg, *Hitler's Germany: Origins, Interpretations, Legacies*, 2d ed. (New York: Routledge, 2009), 301. See also Richard J. Evans, *In Hitler's Dark Shadow: West German Historians and the Attempt to Escape from the Nazi Past* (New York: Pantheon Books, 1989).

44. George Orwell, *Animal Farm* (New York: Signet, 2004); C. L. R. James, *World Revolution 1917–1936: The Rise and Fall of the Communist International* (Atlantic Highlands, NJ: Humanities Press, 1993); Leon Trotsky, *The Revolution Betrayed: What Is the Soviet Union and Where Is It Going?* (New York: Pathfinder Press, 1973); Roy Medvedev, *Let History Judge: The Origins and Consequences of Stalinism* (New York: Columbia University Press, 1989); Arno J. Mayer, *The Furies: Violence and Terror in the French and Russian Revolutions* (Princeton, NJ: Princeton University Press, 2000); Moshe Lewin, *Soviet Century* (London: Verso, 2005); David Priestland, *The Red Flag: A History of Communism* (New York: Grove Press, 2010).

45. Stephane Courtois, Nicolas Werth, Jean-Louis Panne, Andrzej Packowski, and Jean-Louis Margolin, *The Black Book of Communism: Crimes, Terror, Repression* (Cambridge, MA: Harvard University Press, 1999), xviii, xix, 4. Portions of this paragraph draw from Paul Le Blanc, *Marx, Lenin and the Revolutionary Experience: Studies of Communism and Radicalism in the Age of Globalization* (New York: Routledge, 2006), 11–12.

46. Mike Davis, *Late Victorian Holocausts: El Niño Famines and the Making of the Third World* (London: Verso, 2002), 7; Adam Hochschild, *King Leopold's Ghost: A Story of Greed, Terror, and Heroism in Colonial Africa* (Boston: Houghton Mifflin, 2002), 3; John Newsinger, *The Blood Never Dried: A People's History of the British Empire* (London: Bookmarks, 2006), 1. For related material, see George Padmore, *How Britain Rules Africa* (New York: Lothrop, Lee and Shepard, 1936); Kumar Goshal, *People in Colonies* (New York: Sheridan House, 1948); V. G. Kiernan, *The Lords of Human Kind* (London: Century Hutchinson, 1988).

47. Louis Fischer, *The Soviets in World Affairs*, vol. 1 (Princeton, NJ: Princeton University Press, 1951), 151–52, 155, 164–66; International Red Aid, *Fifteen Years of White Terror* (Paris: Les Editions du Secors Rouge Internationale, 1935). Also see F. L. Carsten, *The Rise of Fascism* (Berkeley: University of California Press, 1982); and especially on German fascism, see Stackelberg, *Hitler's Germany*; Arno J. Mayer, *Why Did the Heavens Not Darken? The "Final Solution" in History* (New York: Pantheon Books, 1988); and Franz Neumann, *Behemoth: The Structure and Practice of National Socialism 1933–1944* (New York: Harper and Row, 1966).

48. Luxemburg, "The Crisis of German Social Democracy," 204, 212–13.

49. Ernest Mandel, *The Meaning of the Second World War* (London: Verso, 1986), 169.

50. Heinz Gollwitzer, *Europe in the Age of Imperialism* (New York: W. W. Norton, 1969), 64, 76–77, 81.

51. Bowle, *The Imperial Achievement*, 360.

52. Bowle, *The Imperial Achievement*, 361.

53. Bowle, *The Imperial Achievement*, 362.

54. Christopher Hitchens, *Blood, Class and Empire: The Enduring Anglo-American Relationship* (New York: Nation Books, 2004); William Appleman Williams, *The Tragedy of American Diplomacy* (New York: W. W. Norton, 2009); William Blum, *Killing Hope: U.S. Military and CIA Intervention since World War II* (Monroe, ME: Common Courage Press, 1995); Stephen Kinzer, *Overthrow: America's Century of Regime Change From Hawaii to Iraq* (New York: Henry Holt, 2006); Jeremy Scahill, *Dirty Wars: The World Is a Battlefield* (New York: Nation Books, 2013); Naomi Klein, *The Shock Doctrine: The Rise of Disaster Capitalism* (New York: Picador/Henry Holt, 2008); Betsey Rakocy, Alejandro Reuss, and Chris Sturr, eds., *Real World Globalization: A Reader in Business, Economics and Politics* (Boston: Dollars and Sense, 2007).

55. Paul Sweezy, *The Theory of Capitalist Development* (New York: Monthly Review Press, 1968); Paul Baran, *The Political Economy of Growth* (New York: Monthly Review Press, 1968); Paul Baran and Paul Sweezy, *Monopoly Capital: An Essay on the American Economic and Social Order* (New York: Monthly Review Press, 1964); Harry Magdoff, *Imperialism, From the Colonial Age to the Present* (New York: Monthly Review Press, 1978); Samir Amin, *Accumulation on a World Scale* (New York: Monthly Review Press, 1974); John Bellamy Foster, *Naked Imperialism: The U.S. Pursuit of Global Dominance* (New York: Monthly Review Press, 2007); Alex Callinicos, *Imperialism and the Global Political Economy* (Cambridge, UK: Polity Press, 2009); Immanuel Wallerstein, *The Essential Wallerstein* (New York: The New Press, 2000).

56. David Harvey, *The New Imperialism* (Oxford, UK: Oxford University Press, 2005); Riccardo Bellafiore, ed., *Rosa Luxemburg and the Critique of Political Economy* (New York/London: Routledge, 2013); Riccardo Bellafiore, Ewa Karwoski, and Jan Toporwowski, eds., *The Legacy of Rosa Luxemburg, Oskar Lange, and Michal Kalecki: Essays in Honor of Tadeusz Kowalik*, 2 vols. (New York: Palgrave Macmillan, 2013).

57. Luxemburg, *The Accumulation of Capital*, in *The Complete Works of Rosa Luxemburg*, vol. 2, 325.

58. Georg Adler, Peter Hudis, and Annelies Laschitza, eds., *The Letters of Rosa Luxemburg* (London: Verso, 2011), 457.

59. Adler, Hudis, and Laschitza, *Letters of Rosa Luxembrug*, 375–76.

60. George Orwell, *Nineteen Eighty-Four* in Irving Howe, ed., *Orwell's Nineteen Eighty-Four: Text, Sources, Criticism* (New York: Harcourt, Brace and World, 1963), 118.

61. Orwell, *Nineteen Eighty-Four*, 96.

62. Luxemburg, "The Crisis of German Social Democracy (The Junius Pamphlet)," 209–10.

63. Harvey, *The New Imperialism*, 139–41.

64. Harvey, *The New Imperialism*, 231.

65. See Patrick Bond and Ana Garcial, eds., *BRICS, An Anti-Capitalist Critique* (Chicago: Haymarket Books, 2015); also see Richard Smith, "Creative Destruction: Capitalist Development and China's Environment," *New Left Review* 1, no.

222 (March–April 1997); Kerryn Higgs, *Collision Course: Endless Growth on a Finite Planet* (Cambridge, MA: MIT Press, 2014); Naomi Klein, *This Changes Everything: Capitalism vs. the Climate* (New York: Simon and Schuster, 2015); and the special issue on "The New Imperialism—Globalized Monopoly Capital," *Monthly Review* 67, no. 3 (July–August 2015).

66. Portions of this paragraph are drawn from the essay "Lenin's Return" in Paul Le Blanc, *Unfinished Leninism: The Rise and Return of a Revolutionary Doctrine* (Chicago: Haymarket Books, 2014), 8.

67. From Marge Piercy, "The Consumer," in *Living in the Open* (New York: Alfred A. Knopf, 1976), 77.

68. Frederic Jameson, "Future City," *New Left Review*, no. 21 (May–June 2003): 76. Pushing in the direction of Luxemburg's hopeful appeals are Paul Mason, *Live Working or Die Fighting* (Chicago: Haymarket Books, 2006) and *Why It's Still Taking Off Everywhere* (London: Verso, 2013); and Colin Barker, Laurence Cox, John Krinsky, and Alf Gunvald Nilsen, eds., *Marxism and Social Movements* (Chicago: Haymarket Books, 2013).

CELEBRATING ROSA LUXEMBURG'S LETTERS

1.   Rosa Luxemburg, *The Letters of Rosa Luxemburg*, edited by Georg Adler, Peter Hudis, and Annelies Laschitza (London: Verso, 2011). In my original comments, I concluded my comments with this paragraph.

2.   Rosa Luxemburg, "Reform or Revolution," in *Rosa Luxemburg Speaks*, edited by Mary-Alice Waters (New York: Pathfinder Press, 1970), 39, 87.

3.   Luxemburg, *The Letters of Rosa Luxemburg*, 306, 308.

4.   Luxemburg, *The Letters of Rosa Luxemburg*, 270.

5.   Luxemburg, *The Letters of Rosa Luxemburg*, 298.

6.   Luxemburg, *The Letters of Rosa Luxemburg*, 298.

7.   Luxemburg, *The Letters of Rosa Luxemburg*, 378.

8.   Luxemburg, *The Letters of Rosa Luxemburg*, 409.

9.   Luxemburg, *The Letters of Rosa Luxemburg*, 409.

10. Influential interpretations are reflected in John Weeks, "Imperialism and the World Market," and Ben Fine, "Primitive Accumulation," both in Tom Bottomore, Laurence Harris, V. G. Kiernan, and Ralph Miliband, eds., *A Dictionary of Marxist Thought*, 2d ed. (Oxford, UK and Cambridge, MA: Blackwell, 1991), 252–56 and 444–45. Luxemburg's divergence from this is discussed in Paul Le Blanc, "Introduction: Rosa Luxemburg and the Global Violence of Capitalism," in *The Complete Works of Rosa Luxemburg*, vol. 2, edited by Peter Hudis and Paul Le Blanc (London: Verso, 2015), xv–xvi, xix–xxiv.

11. Rosa Luxemburg, "The Crisis in the German Social Democracy (The Junius Pamphlet)," in *Rosa Luxemburg Speaks*, 269.

12. Paul Frölich, *Rosa Luxemburg: Her Life and Work* (New York: Monthly Review Press, 1972), 182.

COMIC BOOK ROSA

1. Helen C. Scott and Paul Le Blanc, "Introduction to Rosa Luxemburg," in *Socialism or Barbarism: The Selected Writings of Rosa Luxemburg*, edited by Paul Le Blanc and Helen C. Scott (London: Pluto Press, 2010), 3.

2. From Zetkin's obituary for Luxemburg, quoted in Tony Cliff, "Introduction," in Paul Frölich, *Rosa Luxemburg: Her Life and Work* (New York: Monthly Review Press, 1972), xi.

ROSA LUXEMBURG FOR OUR OWN TIME: STRUGGLES FOR REFORM AND REVOLUTION IN THE FACE OF CAPITAL ACCUMULATION

1. See Helen C. Scott and Paul Le Blanc, "Introduction to Rosa Luxemburg," in *Socialism or Barbarism: The Selected Writings of Rosa Luxemburg*, edited by Paul Le Blanc and Helen C. Scott (London: Pluto Press, 2010), 3–35.

2. This phrase sticks in my mind as something Lars said, although (since I am unable to find it in his published work) it may only have been in discussion at a conference or in an email. It is consistent, however, with how both he and I see the matter. See, for example, Lars Lih, "Lenin and Kautsky," *International Socialist Review*, no. 59 (May–June 2008), isreview.org, and Paul Le Blanc, "Lenin's Marxism," *Platypus Review*, no. 35 (May 2011), platypus1917.org.

3. See Paul Le Blanc, "Luxemburg and Lenin Through Each Other's Eyes," *Links, International Journal of Socialist Renewal* (January 3, 2012), links.org.

4. Luxemburg, "Mass Strike, Political Party and Trade Unions," in *Socialism or Barbarism*, 116–17.

5. V. I. Lenin, "What Is To Be Done?" in *Revolution, Democracy, Socialism: Selected Writings*, edited by Paul Le Blanc (London: Pluto Press, 2008), 138.

6. N. K. Krupskaya, *Reminiscences of Lenin* (New York: International Publishers, 1970), 167.

7. Luxemburg, "Reform or Revolution?" in *Socialism or Barbarism*, 48.

8. Berten quoted in Mary Nolan, *Social Democracy and Society: Working-Class Radicalism in Dusseldorf, 1890–1920* (New York: Cambridge University Press, 1981), 243.

9. Rosa Luxemburg, "Eight Hour Day at the Party Congress" (1902), and "Down with Reformist Illusions—Hail the Revolutionary Class Struggle!" (1913). Both can be found in the Marxist Internet Archive.

10. Two valuable discussions of current realities can be found in Paul Mason, *Why It's Still Kicking Off Everywhere: The New Global Revolutions* (London: Verso, 2013), and Luke Cooper and Simon Hardy, *Beyond Capitalism? The Future of Radical Politics* (Winchester, UK: Zero Books, 2012).

11. Lenin, "The Revolutionary Proletariat and the Rights of Nations to Self-Determination," in *Revolution, Democracy, Socialism*, 233–34.

12. Luxemburg, "The Russian Revolution," in *Socialism or Barbarism*, 225–37.

13. Harry Magdoff, *Imperialism: From the Colonial Age to the Present* (New York:

Monthly Review Press, 1978), 260–61. See portions of Lenin's *Imperialism, the Highest Stage of Capitalism* contained in *Revolution, Socialism, Democracy,* 236–49; see also Phil Gasper, ed., *Imperialism and War: Classic Writings by Lenin and Bukharin* (Chicago: Haymarket Books, 2017).

14. Daniel Gaido and Manuel Quiroga, "The Early Reception of Rosa Luxemburg's Theory of Imperialism," *Capital & Class* 37, no. 3 (2014): 450–51.

15. Rosa Luxemburg, *The Accumulation of Capital* (London: Routledge and Kegan Paul, 1951), 370–72.

16. Luxemburg, *The Accumulation of Capital,* 376.

17. David Harvey, *The New Imperialism* (New York: Oxford University Press, 2005), 140–42.

18. Luxemburg, *The Accumulation of Capital,* 365–66.

19. David Harvey, *Rebel Cities: From the Right to the City to the Urban Revolution* (London: Verso, 2013), 23.

20. Karl Marx and Frederick Engels, *Manifesto of the Communist Party,* in Karl Marx and Frederick Engels, *Selected Works,* vol. 1 (Moscow: Progress Publishers, 1973), 126.

21. Luxemburg, *The Accumulation of Capital,* 351–52. This good point is made by Peter Hudis in a paper presented to the Rethinking Marxism Conference, September 2013: "The Dialectic of the Spatial Determination of Capital: Rosa Luxemburg's *Accumulation of Capital* Reconsidered."

QUESTIONS AND REFLECTIONS

1. This is the first entry in the present volume, which first appeared in Volume 5 of *The International Encyclopedia of Revolution and Protest, 1500 to Present,* 8 vols., edited by Immanuel Ness (Malden, MA and Oxford, UK: Wiley-Blackwell, 2009).

2. The article is available in the Marxist Internet Archive: marxists.org/archive/luxemburg/1906/06/blanquism.html.

3. Examples of Serge's valuable contributions (in addition to such novels as *Conquered City, Midnight in the Century,* and *The Case of Comrade Tulayev*) include *From Lenin to Stalin* (New York: Pathfinder Press, 1973) and *Memoirs of a Revolutionary* (New York: New York Review of Books, 2012).

4. Marcel van der Linden, *Western Marxism and the Soviet Union* (Chicago: Haymarket Books, 2009).

5. C. L. R. James, *State Capitalism and World Revolution,* written in collaboration with Raya Dunayevskaya and Grace Lee (Chicago: Charles H. Kerr, 1986). Much of the "precision" referred to here can be found in the work of James's collaborator: Raya Dunayevskaya, *Russia: from Proletarian Revolution to State-Capitalist Counter-Revolution, Selected Writings,* edited by Eugene Gogol and Franklin Dmitryev (Chicago: Haymarket Books, 2018).

6. On this question, see Joseph Hansen, *Dynamics of the Cuban Revolution* (New York: Pathfinder Press, 1979); Janette Habel, *Cuba: The Revolution in Peril* (London: Verso, 1991); and Paul Le Blanc, "Origins and Trajectory of the Cuban

Revolution," *Revolutionary Studies: Essays in Plain Marxism* (Chicago: Haymarket Books, 2017), 131–44.

WHY SHOULD WE CARE WHAT ROSA LUXEMBURG THOUGHT?

1. C. Wright Mills, *The Marxists* (New York: Dell, 1962), 149.
2. Hannah Arendt, "Rosa Luxemburg (1871–1919)," in *Men in Dark Times* (New York: Harcourt, Brace and World, 1968), 37.
3. Arendt, "Rosa Luxemburg (1871–1919)," 37.
4. Arendt, "Rosa Luxemburg (1871–1919)," 56.
5. Stephen Eric Bronner, *Rosa Luxemburg: A Revolutionary for Our Times* (University Park: Pennsylvania State Press, 1997); Stephen Eric Bronner, ed., *The Letters of Rosa Luxemburg* (Atlantic Highlands, NJ: Humanities Press, 1993); Stephen Eric Bronner, ed., *Socialism in History: Political Essays of Henry Pachter* (New York: Columbia University Press, 1984).
6. Stephen Eric Bronner, "Red Dreams and the New Millennium: Notes on the Legacy of Rosa Luxemburg," in *Rosa Luxemburg: Her Life and Legacy,* edited by Jason Schulman (New York: Palgrave Macmillan, 2013), 11–19. This essay, and others referred to (plus the present contribution) originally appeared as part of a running discussion/debate in the socialist journal *New Politics.* These were gathered in the volume edited by Schulman.
7. Alan Johnson, "A Critical Reply to Stephen Eric Bronner," David Camfield, "A Second Reply to Stephen Eric Bronner," Stephen Eric Bronner, "Rosa Redux: A Reply to David Camfield and Alan Johnson," in Schulman, *Rosa Luxemburg,* 21–37, 39–47, 49–71.
8. Bronner, "Rosa Redux," 60.
9. Paul Le Blanc, *From Marx to Gramsci: A Reader in Revolutionary Marxist Politics,* 2d ed. (Chicago: Haymarket Books, 2016); Paul Le Blanc, *Lenin and the Revolutionary Party* (New York: Humanity Books, 1993); and Paul Le Blanc, ed., *Rosa Luxemburg: Reflections and Writings* (New York: Humanity Books, 1999).
10. Schulman, *Rosa Luxemburg,* 53.
11. Schulman, 18. This version of Bronner's essay omits the references to Rwanda and Sierra Leone contained in the earlier *New Politics* version.
12. Schulman, *Rosa Luxemburg,* 67.
13. Schulman, *Rosa Luxemburg,* 12, 16, 18, 19.
14. Schulman, *Rosa Luxemburg,* 17.
15. Schulman, *Rosa Luxemburg,* 34.
16. Schulman, *Rosa Luxemburg,* 44–45.
17. Schulman, *Rosa Luxemburg,* 17.
18. Schulman, *Rosa Luxemburg,* 34.

A HUNDRED YEARS AFTER HER DEATH

1. Bertolt Brecht, "Epitaph 1919," quoted in Wendy Forrest, *Rosa Luxemburg* (London: Hamish Hamilton, 1989), 61.

2. Stephen Eric Bronner, ed., *The Letters of Rosa Luxemburg*, New Edition (Atlantic Highlands: Humanities Press, 1993), 60.

3. Quoted in Paul Frölich, *Rosa Luxemburg: Her Life and Work*, translated by Johanna Hoornweg (New York: Monthly Review Press, 1972), 189.

4. Bronner, *The Letters of Rosa Luxemburg*, 60.

5. Bronner, *The Letters of Rosa Luxemburg*, 77–78.

6. Max Adler, quoted in Frölich, *Rosa Luxemburg*, 197.

7. Frölich, *Rosa Luxemburg*, 182.

8. Luxemburg, "Reform or Revolution," in *Rosa Luxemburg Speaks*, edited by Mary-Alice Waters (New York: Pathfinder Press, 1970), 36

9. Luxemburg, "Organizational Question of Social Democracy," 129.

10. Luxemburg, "The Mass Strike," 176.

11. Luxemburg, "The Mass Strike," 176.

12. Luxemburg, "The Mass Strike," 200.

13. Rosa Luxemburg, *The Accumulation of Capital* (London: Routledge and Kegan Paul), 454.

14. Luxemburg, *The Accumulation of Capital*, 455.

15. Rosa Luxemburg, "The Crisis in the German Social Democracy (The Junius Pamphlet)," 269: "either an advance to socialism or a reversion to barbarism."

16. Rosa Luxemburg, Karl Liebknecht, Klara Zetkin, and Franz Mehring, "A Call to the Workers of the World (November 1918)," https://www.marxists.org/archive/luxemburg/1918/11/25.htm.

17. Luxemburg, "The Russian Revolution," *Rosa Luxemburg Speaks*, 375.

18. Luxemburg, "The Russian Revolution," 393–94.

19. Rosa Luxemburg, "Order Prevails in Berlin," in *Socialism or Barbarism: The Selected Writings of Rosa Luxemburg*, edited by Paul Le Blanc and Helen C. Scott (London: Pluto Press, 2010), 267.

INDEX

"Passim" (literally "scattered") indicates intermittent discussion of a topic over a cluster of pages.

ABOUT THE AUTHOR

PAUL LE BLANC is a professor of history at La Roche College, has written on and participated in the US labor, radical, and civil rights movements, and is author of such books as *Marx, Lenin, and the Revolutionary Experience*, *A Short History of the U.S. Working Class*, and *Work and Struggle: Voices from U.S. Labor Radicalism*. In addition, he has coauthored, with economist Michael Yates, the highly acclaimed *A Freedom Budget for All Americans: Recapturing the Promise of the Civil Rights Movement in the Struggle for Economic Justice Today*.

ABOUT HAYMARKET BOOKS

Haymarket Books is a radical, independent, nonprofit book publisher based in Chicago.

Our mission is to publish books that contribute to struggles for social and economic justice. We strive to make our books a vibrant and organic part of social movements and the education and development of a critical, engaged, international left.

We take inspiration and courage from our namesakes, the Haymarket martyrs, who gave their lives fighting for a better world. Their 1886 struggle for the eight-hour day—which gave us May Day, the international workers' holiday—reminds workers around the world that ordinary people can organize and struggle for their own liberation. These struggles continue today across the globe—struggles against oppression, exploitation, poverty, and war.

Since our founding in 2001, Haymarket Books has published more than five hundred titles. Radically independent, we seek to drive a wedge into the risk-averse world of corporate book publishing. Our authors include Noam Chomsky, Arundhati Roy, Rebecca Solnit, Angela Y. Davis, Howard Zinn, Amy Goodman, Wallace Shawn, Mike Davis, Winona LaDuke, Ilan Pappé, Richard Wolff, Dave Zirin, Keeanga-Yamahtta Taylor, Nick Turse, Dahr Jamail, David Barsamian, Elizabeth Laird, Amira Hass, Mark Steel, Avi Lewis, Naomi Klein, and Neil Davidson. We are also the trade publishers of the acclaimed Historical Materialism Book Series and of Dispatch Books.